FAITH TALK

Faith Talk

WITH HEATHER HART

& CONTRIBUTING AUTHORS

Faith Talk: Christian Women & The Gospel
Copyright © 2010, 2020 Heather Hart and Contributing Authors

ISBN: 9798477733521

Edited by Valerie Riese
Cover design by Heather Hart
Cover photo © Africa Studio—Stock.Adobe.com

Visit Candidly Christian online to learn more at CandidlyChristian.com

TABLE OF CONTENTS

Part Two

INTRODUCTION

Heather Hart

If I asked you to tell me why Jesus matters, what would you say?

If we were in the same room, eye contact would have just gone out the window. You may fidget a bit or give me a deer-in-the-headlights kind of look. Someone might respond with one of those safe, Sunday school answers. You know, "because He's God," or "He's our Lord and Savior." However, if we were to press deeper, it would get a little bit harder.

Several years ago, I asked a group of women the following question: "What is the gospel?" Some of them were very confident in their answers: "The gospel is the good news."

Remember when we were kids, and we would repeatedly ask our parents why? Or maybe you weren't as annoying as I was, but you have seen TV shows where kids do so? I was one of those kids. So, you can probably guess what came next. I asked them what the "good news" was.

We didn't drill it down as far as we could have, and I didn't ask to make them feel bad. I wasn't even sure I had a better answer myself. These women had all been Christians longer than I had been alive. They knew their faith. What I really wanted to accomplish was to acknowledge there was a gap in our faith talk.

In all our Bible studies, conferences, Sunday school lessons, sermons, and even the everyday conversations we have about Jesus, it seems like the very cornerstone of our faith is missing. The gospel is the foundation of our faith, it's centered on Jesus, yet somehow, we have put them on the back burner.

In 2019, The Gospel Coalition published an article that took this a step further. The author, Erik Raymond, revealed what people who leave the Christian faith don't say. He did such a good job; I want to share his words with you here:

"The truth is, people don't often turn away from the faith and talk much about Jesus. He is neither impugned nor discredited.

They may talk about the church. They may wince at the Bible's teaching. They may talk about their personal journey.

But Jesus?

He remains as he was before Pilate.

Even though he is central to the whole discussion, people seem content to look right past him. Like Pilate, they wash their hands of him and add, by their silence, "I find no guilt in him.[1]"[2]

Think about that for a moment.

Have you seen that to be true?

I have. And I think the way to counteract it is to start making more of Jesus. To stop assuming Jesus and the gospel are common knowledge and start talking about them. That's what *Faith Talk* is all about.

---

[1] Luke 23:4

[2] Raymond, Erik. "What Apostates Don't Say." The Gospel Coalition, August 22, 2019. https://www.thegospelcoalition.org/blogs/erik-raymond/apostates-dont-say/. (Accessed March 4th, 2020.)

PART ONE
LET'S TALK ABOUT FAITH

Chapter 1

Let's Talk About It

Heather Hart

In June 2020, Christian author, Traci Rhoades, posted the following question on Twitter: "One sentence—what is the gospel of Jesus Christ?" Over 150 people took up the challenge. There was everything from one-word answers to run-on sentences to song lyrics. Life, love, salvation, hope, truth, everlasting...

Trying to squeeze the gospel into less than 280 characters is hard. Narrowing it down to one sentence is nearly impossible. There were a lot of correct answers, but not a lot of answers that would mean anything to someone who wasn't already a follower of Christ.

The gospel is life altering. It is literally translated as the "good news." However, all too often, I demote it to an idea—a doctrine. I try to whittle it down to a concept instead of the merciful, loving, life-giving, mind-blowing grace of an almighty God.

Yes, I could see God in the answers on Twitter. I know God is love. He is truth. And He is gracious. But the gospel is more than that. The good news Jesus came to give us has the power to transform us. The gospel is the story of a holy God who loves us enough to pursue us, no matter what we've done, regardless of what it costs Him. And it cost Him everything.

THE GOOD NEWS

In the beginning, God created the heavens and the earth. He created the birds of the air and the fish in the sea. The plants and animals, all of it was created by God. Including man.

God placed a man named Adam in a garden called Eden with a wife named Eve. God gave them one clear-cut rule: You can eat fruit from any tree in the garden except one.

You know what it's like to have something off limits, right? It makes it even more tempting. So, when Satan reared his ugly little head for the first time, Adam and Even were ready to take a bite. They broke God's one and only rule; they sinned.

The Bible defines sin in James 4:17 as not doing the right thing. "So whoever knows the right thing to do and fails to do it, for him it is sin." Have you ever failed to do the right thing? I know I have. And here's the kicker: The punishment for sin is death. It's separation from God for eternity in a place often referred to as hell or *Sheol*. I don't want to get all fire and brimstone on you, but there is a real eternal life at stake here–yours. That's the bad news, but what I really want to tell you the good news about God's love, because it's so much bigger than His wrath.

God loves the people of the world so much that He sent His Son, Jesus, to live a perfect life, and die a sinner's death—beaten and alone—so we could be forgiven. He was hung on a cross and buried in a tomb, but on the third day, He rose again, and He still lives today. I know He does, because His Spirit lives in my heart, and He can live in your heart, too. His death and resurrection made it possible for us to have a relationship with the God who created our universe. By His blood we are forgiven, and because of it, nothing separates us from Him.

Throughout this book, you're going to read stories from women who are living with Jesus every day. The first part of this book is full of women sharing how the gospel changed their life. How they found Jesus. In part two, you'll read how the gospel continues to work in their lives each and every day.

I wanted to start this book by sharing my mother's testimony. Her search for God was just that, a search. It's a story of God wooing her to Himself. She was seeking Jesus... and she found Him. But I'll let her tell the story...

WHAT AM I MISSING?

Barbara Ford

Growing up, I remember feeling like life was pointless; like there was no purpose. I felt like God created me; I just had no idea who God was. My older sister took me to church and gave me a Bible when I was in junior high school. At church, I heard nice stories and a lot of rules. "Be good and go to church" was the takeaway I got from that experience.

I read the King James Bible my sister gave me cover to cover. And I closed the Bible with no answers to the questions I was asking.

So, I kept reading.

I read a lot about religious people and different faiths, including missionaries, mythology, Muslims, and Buddhist, but I still didn't find what I was looking for. My experiences at churches and Christian organizations all felt rules-based and social. Yet the Bible was the one thing that kept calling me back. Somewhere deep inside, I knew the Bible held the key.

In my first year of college, I heard about The Living Bible and got a copy. I found it spoke to my soul in a way the King James Bible never did. The two said the same thing (I checked), but The Living Bible was different; less formal and easier to understand. It was like it was written just for me.

I remember reading the Old Testament and wondering how to become Jewish. I wanted to know the God of Abraham, Isaac, and Jacob. But then I got to the Gospels, and that's where I met Jesus.

Jesus said, "I am the Way—yes, and the Truth and the Life. No one can get to the Father except by means of me." [1] I was sure that was God, and that's what I needed. I needed Jesus.

When I got to The Book of Acts, I read about Philip witnessing to the Eunuch and baptizing him. I knew baptism needed to be my next step. So, I pulled out a phone book and looked at the list of churches; searching for one that would baptize me by immersion like the Eunuch. I needed my sins to be washed away.

After finding one, I went on Sunday, responded to the alter call, and was baptized shortly thereafter. But I knew that wasn't the end. I wanted to learn more. Not more head knowledge, but how to have a relationship with Christ... However, I had no idea what that looked like.

I knew Jesus. I knew I was saved. Yet I had no idea what to do with that. No idea where to go from there.

Despite their best efforts, the church I was going to did nothing to help me grow in my faith. Few college kids went to the church, so the church created a college class for my friends and me. They taught us all about the history of

---

[1] John 14:6

Christianity. It was highly informative, but it didn't teach me anything about living for Christ.

So, I started church hopping. I tried several denominations: Methodist, Quaker, Presbyterian, Baptist, etc. At each one, it was always the same. There was a lot of information about church, but nothing about Jesus.

Eventually, I stopped searching for a church. I kept reading my Bible because Jesus was there on the pages. I just didn't know how to find Him in life. I didn't even know what I was looking for, really. I just knew I wasn't finding it.

It was years before I started attending church regularly. There was a church in my area I drove past frequently, so I went one Sunday. As soon as I walked in the door, I knew something was different. After forty years of searching, I felt at home.

I was met with smiles and friendly greetings. The comfortable setting was welcoming; however, it was the sermon that kept me coming back. The pastor shared the gospel in a way I understood. He talked about the Jesus I already knew.

Someone encouraged me to come to Sunday school and on Wednesday nights. The teaching was sound and built on Christ alone. Moreover, I wanted to be there. I became part of their church family in a way I didn't know existed, and I've never looked back.

Jesus changed my life. Our journey isn't over, but I finally feel like I have a good foundation of faith. And I'm part of a family of believers. Their fellowship, their encouragement, their prayers, they don't just have something different about them, they are sharing the light of Christ with the world and with others. And I have it, too. I finally have what I was looking for my whole life. I have a relationship with Jesus and the Holy Spirit living inside me.

LET'S TALK ABOUT FAITH

1. How can you put the gospel into words?

2. Does your church family help you grow in your walk with God?

3. How could you relate to Barb's testimony?

THE GOOD NEWS

The Bible is living and active, and it has the power to transform our lives. It tells us about a God who created us, loves us, and wants to intimately know us on a personal level.

CHAPTER 2

THE FACTS OF LIFE

Heather Hart

On August 12th in 1936, it reached 120 degrees in the small Texas town where I live. That date etched our community into history as the state record holder of the hottest town in Texas. A record our community fully embraced, making our town slogan, "We're hotter than you are."

It's fun to joke about, but the Texas heat isn't always fun and games. Especially when you are the one paying the air conditioning bill. However, I shared this for another reason.

Before I moved to this small town, before I even knew of its existence, I attended a church camp one summer that changed my life. Something the speaker said that year reminds me of our town slogan.

It was a fun little back-and-forth thing he did with us to make sure we were paying attention. You know how those go: he says something, we say something back, then he says something else. We repeated the exercise countless times that week. It went a little something like this...

Speaker: "Jalapeño."

Us: "Whoa, that's hot."

Speaker: "Yes, it is, but hell's hotter."

The back-and-forth routine didn't save my soul. I don't even remember what he actually spoke about. What I do remember is that somewhere between the jalapeños, mini golf, new friends, and cafeteria food, I met Jesus that week at camp.

It wasn't that I hadn't heard about Jesus before. Quite the contrary. I was raised in the church. We lived next door to a church when I was little, and we were there every Sunday. My earliest memories are of my mom preparing to teach Sunday school lessons.

All my summers growing up were filled with vacation Bible school and various church camps. And they were awesome. I loved them.

I believed everything the Bible said. If you would have asked me, I would have said I was a Christian. I believed in God. I knew Jesus died on the cross and rose again. I knew it was because we were sinners in need of a savior. But here's the thing... to me, the crucifixion—the death and resurrection of Jesus—was just a fact of life that I assumed everyone knew. The sky is blue, the grass is green, and God created the heavens and the earth. Snow is cold, trees have leaves, and Jesus died for you and me. These facts meant nothing to me; they were just head knowledge. I knew they were true, but that was it.

I guess you could say going to church was no different to me than going to Girl Scouts; we even used the same building. I mean, at Wednesday night church we talked about Jesus, and at Girl Scouts we earned badges, so they served a different purpose. But beyond that, I got to hang out with my friends in a small group setting and it was a ton of fun. We either learned about God or learned a life skill. In both scenarios, I was happy.

Then, that summer at church camp, everything changed. I went to church camp every summer, but I should clarify— I went to a different church camp each summer. My church didn't have a camp. By the time I was in middle school, I didn't even really have a church. When of my friends invited me, I would go with them. That's what happened in the summer between eighth and ninth grade.

It was 1998 and my best friend invited me to go to camp with her. It was a camp that lasted for a whole week, and it had a ton of rules. Like there was a dress code, and we weren't allowed to cuss. So, we spent weeks preparing for camp.

I don't know if our preparation made a difference or not, but this camp was nothing like I had ever experienced before. It wasn't just arts and crafts, Bible lessons, and singing; it was a full-blown church camp. There was a lake where we went canoeing, a mini golf course, a swimming pool, and we had Bible study and worship services multiple times a day.

During one service, I learned you could have a personal relationship with Jesus. I learned He wasn't just a fact of life. That Jesus wasn't just something you learned about at church, but living and active *and* He wanted to be a part of my life.

That realization changed everything for me.

I came home from church camp a completely different person than I was when I left. I was on fire for Christ in a way I didn't even know was possible.

As I went back to the real world, I learned how to let Jesus soak into every aspect of my life. Jesus was no longer a fact or a footnote. He was my best friend.

LET'S TALK ABOUT FAITH

1. Have you ever felt like God was just a fact, but nothing personal?

2. Do you have a personal relationship with Jesus?

3. How could you relate to Heather's testimony?

THE GOOD NEWS

The gospel isn't just a word or a fact, it's being loved by a God who wants to know you personally.

CHAPTER 3

A CANDID SALVATION STORY

Valerie Riese

> "The greatest among you will be your servant.
> For those who exalt themselves will be humbled,
> and those who humble themselves will be exalted."
> ~ Matthew 23:11-12, NIV

It had reached ninety degrees before noon all week, but I was determined to go for a bike ride. I left with a piece of toast in my mouth and headed out of town toward the solace of farmland. My entire body exhaled as car horns faded to crow calls and I pedaled harder.

Just a few months before, my neurologist declared the rare brain disease I'd struggled with for almost four years was in remission. Despite scars of anxiety, compromised vision, and cognitive damage, I thanked God for another pain-free morning.

Determined to get stronger, I pedaled through one country mile after another. The sun hung over my shoulder as I stopped to wipe the sweat raining from my forehead. Suddenly I realized that however far I rode, I also had to ride the same distance back home.

I rationed one drink of warm water at each stop sign. Still four miles from home, I leaned back and tapped the bottom of the bottle to get every sacred drop. My head spun and panic creeped in as I prayed "Oh, no!, Please God, no. Not here..."

I opened my eyes to see truck tires whiz by. Then I heard it stop, and slowly the tires came back into view. As I wondered why I was laying in the gravel, a man's manure-covered boots stepped out of the truck and walked toward me. My heart raced as I peeled my face from the gravel to find my hair, and all the way down my side, covered with chunks of half-digested toast.

> "And if anyone gives even a cup of cold water to one of these little ones who is my disciple, truly I tell you, that person will certainly not lose their reward."
> ~ Matthew 10:42, NIV

The old man looked just as scared and confused as I was. He ran back to the truck, came back and kneeled down in front of me. Then he slowly reached toward my sticky face with all he had—one small paper towel. Still unable to speak, my thoughts protested, Oh no! I'm so gross! You can't clean me with that! Who does that...?! Who are you—*Jesus*?!

As he gently wiped my cheek, I looked up, made eye contact, and that's exactly who I saw.

I've never seen such unblemished liquid love in the eyes of a total stranger. The old farmer didn't care who I was, how disgusting I looked, or why I was lying alone on the side of the road covered in my own vomit. He saw another human being in need of help and did what he could with all that he had.

He told me his daughter-in-law was nearby and promised to come back. He jumped in the truck and a few minutes later, a young woman with a warm smile invited me into her car, assuring me it was no big deal if some of whatever was on my face got on her fabric. She brought me home, made sure my husband was there to care for me, and came back a few minutes later with my bike.

A few days later, I bought a box of chocolate and a card that said "thank you for being my angel" on the cover and a Bible verse on the inside. I didn't know who they were or what they believed, but I knew Jesus was in that man's eyes.

> "The Word of God that I speak from my mouth will not return to Him empty, but will accomplish what He desires and achieve the purpose for which He has sent it to me."
> ~ Isaiah 55:11, NIV

I knocked on the open screen door of the old farmhouse. The same woman who took me home invited me in for lemonade. Scripture painted on the living room archway welcomed me "For I know the plans I have for you," declares the Lord, "plans to prosper you and not to harm you, plans to give you hope and a future" Jeremiah 29:11.[1] The squeak of the screen door closing behind me was drowned out by her squeals as she opened my card: "Oh, we *love* Jesus!"

In that moment, I remembered the pure childlike concern in her father-in-law's eyes, and deep within me, I almost heard a match strike, and a glowing warmth encased my soul.

> "And I will pray the Father, and he shall give you another Comforter, that he may abide with you forever."
> ~ John 14:16, NIV

---

[1] NIV

In the coming weeks, the flame grew warmer and warmer until I thought I would combust. One morning, I burst into tears to my husband yelling, "Something in me is different! I don't know what it is, but all I want is my Bible. I can't stand country music anymore; I only want songs about God. I want to sing about Jesus and listen to sermons. I don't want to just know *of Him* anymore. I want to *know Him* and never look back!"

He looked at me plainly and said "Yeah, so..? Then do it."

This is my salvation story. I've never told it before because it's not glamorous or fancy. But it needs to be told, because it's time to praise the humble. It's time for others to see their good deeds and glorify our Father in heaven.

As I share my salvation story, I realize it's not really my story at all. It's about Jesus saving grace through compassionate service and childlike zeal. The farmer humbled himself to serve a woman passed out in the ditch. His daughter-in-law spontaneously praised her Savior. And Jesus used both of them simply because they were willing and available.

I pray their story will inspire us to do the same.

LET'S TALK ABOUT FAITH

1. How has God used believers to minister to you?

2. Have you ever thought about something as simple as a good deed or thank you note being a platform for talking about Jesus?

3. Have you ever felt like your salvation story was nothing special?

4. Could you relate to Valerie's testimony?

THE GOOD NEWS

We don't have to be important or even feel special for God to love us and pursue a relationship with us. God created us to love us. All our failures and shortcomings are covered by the blood of Christ, who loved us enough to die for us. We are wholly loved.

CHAPTER 4

A FOUNDATION OF TRUTH

Theresa Boedecker

I don't remember a time I didn't believe in God. With childlike faith, I accepted He was important and part of life. Just like I believed everything my parents taught me. Following God provided a rhythm and routine to life. I prayed at night, went to church with my family, took notes during the sermon, and sang with the congregation.

I worked hard to be a good daughter, sister, student, Christian. But while I was busy trying to be good, I absorbed wrong messages about life, myself, and God. I didn't know it, but I was building my life on half-lies that influenced my actions, thoughts, and behavior.

Some lies came from the way my parents raised and treated me. Others came from how I interpreted life and what happened to me. And some came from church.

I attended Bible study and memorized many Scriptures, but I also learned that God made a lot of rules. The church taught many good rules, but also a number of wrong rules. Our church believed in the Bible, God, and Christ, but it focused more on the Old Testament rules and festivals than on the New Testament message. Christ was talked about, but not as the main hero.

The church was works based. We were encouraged to earn our faith and God's love, not to receive them as gifts. We were taught to do for God so He would do for us.

The same went for my mom. My siblings and I had to earn her love and approval, or her displeasure was shown. We were not validated and loved unconditionally. Instead, we were told what to think and feel, and then shown that our feelings, thoughts, and emotions were not important. Her actions taught me I was only important if I was doing the right thing. I had to please her, make her look good, and make the family look good.

When I met my husband, he challenged some of my long-held beliefs. I began listening to Christian radio (something our church never allowed), and I finally realized Christianity was more about a relationship with God than following rules. Wow! That was a mind-blowing concept.

We moved 2000 miles and joined a church that focused on Christ, love, grace, and other things that were new to me. My view of God expanded. I realized He was more loving than I had ever imagined. My distorted view of Him changed.

When I became a mom, I knew I didn't want to raise my children the way I was raised. I was learning about God's unconditional love, and how all His actions are motivated by love for us. That love flows from Him as our loving parent.

I read the Bible and found God's love on every page, and in every story. I could see Him as a perfect, loving father, not the waiting-for-me-to-fail view I had adopted as a child.

Raising my children helped me see that our relationship with Him mirrors our relationship with our children. I loved my children before they were born. I don't make them earn my love. It is a free gift I willingly give. I want what's best for them and am motivated by love. I say no and set boundaries to keep them safe and secure so they feel loved.

I care for all of my children's needs, emotions, thoughts, and feelings. My love does not come and go. I love them even on days they whine and misbehave.

I am generous with them, and am motivated by grace, kindness, and giving. I want to give them the best of everything. I don't want to force them to love me. I don't guilt or scare them into loving me. I want them to naturally and freely love me of their own choice.

If I naturally love and want the best for my children, then how much more does God want this for me?

He is not my mother, my teacher, or the boss I had to please and impress. And I am no longer that little child trying to find the right combination to please everyone. I am not who society tells me I am, or who I think I am, but who God says I am. Beloved. Loved. Cherished. Redeemed. Saved.

Slowly, the lies I believed were smashed by the truth, His truth. Second Corinthians 10:5 says, "We demolish arguments and every pretension that sets itself up against the knowledge of God, and we take captive every thought to make it obedient to Christ."[1] Toppling the enemy's lies with God's truth changed my thoughts and beliefs in three significant ways.

1. I don't have to earn love. God loves me unconditionally, whether I make my bed, get upset with my children, or arrive late for an appointment. His love is a gift, not something I earn or can ever pay back.

2. I matter. My needs, feelings, emotions—all of me matters. God doesn't want me to hide. He wants me to reveal myself to Him. He loves all of me, even my warts, mistakes, and flaws.

3. My worth is based on His view of me, not mine, or the opinions of other people. And it doesn't

---

[1] NIV

fluctuate, depending on the day, my actions, or my attitude.

The gospel impacts my everyday life, how I talk to myself, how I treat others, and how I view the world. I lived much of my childhood in fear, thinking I had to do the right thing and make the right choices or people and God would be angry with me. I saw God as petty, vindictive, and handing out gold stars only when earned. I thought God was a scorekeeper.

Now I see God as loving me unconditionally and giving me the freedom to love Him back. Yes, sin hurts us, those around us, and our relationship with Him, but He loves us, pursues us, and offers the remedy for our sins. Because of this, I can imitate Him by having compassion, showing grace, and offering forgiveness to others. I can see their hurt toward themselves and others as a condition of their heart and view them with love instead of bitterness.

When I realized God does not shame us, guilt us, or punish us into following Him, loving Him, or making right choices, how then could I not do the same for others? The father in the prodigal son story runs to meet his son. He embraces his son in a hug and prepares a feast. He doesn't make him feel guilty for his past decisions. Instead, he embraces his decision to humbly come back to start again.[2]

If God is love and He loves me, then I am to pass His love on and love others. One of my favorite verses is 1 John 4:7-8. "Those who are loved by God, let his love continually pour from you to one another, because God is love. Everyone who loves is fathered by God and experiences an intimate knowledge of him."[3] I am still learning what this means and will be for years.

I am slowly replacing the lies I believed about God, myself, others, and life with the truth of God. His truth

---

[2] Luke 15:11-22
[3] TPT

replaces my lies, wiggles them free from their supports, and brings them crashing down. This freedom affects every aspect of my life.

I imagine the same is true for you, too.

The Bible says the truth shall set us free.[4] And it does.

It will be a lifelong process. Replacing lies with God's truth takes time and examination, but it's worth it. God's truth sets us free, makes us happier, and gives us hope. When we're free, we're more able to love God, others, and ourselves more than we ever thought possible.

LET'S TALK ABOUT FAITH

1. Have you ever felt like you had to earn God's love?

2. What are some lies you have believed about your standing with Jesus?

3. How can you relate to Theresa's testimony?

THE GOOD NEWS

We are more loved than we could ever imagine, and we don't have to do anything to earn it.

---

[4] John 8:32

Chapter 5

The Greatest Adventure

Hadassah Trev

Have you had the feeling that nobody cares, and your life has no meaning and purpose? Have you felt this void in you, full of aching and longing, thirsty for unconditional love and belonging, for something stable and secure?

I felt this way in my teens. Living in an atmosphere of fear because of the abusive behavior of my father, I sank deeper into a pit of depression, self-doubt, and suicidal thoughts. By this time, I had already discovered the huge discrepancy between what I wanted to be and what I was, and my absolute inability to change my condition. I was terrified and ashamed of certain thoughts and actions that I could not change. I wanted to be good, but I couldn't. I wanted to love, but I couldn't. A hurricane of resentment, offense, hatred, and anger raged within me, and I could not control it.

In utter desperation, I cried out to the universe and placed an ultimatum. "God, if you exist, I challenge you to show yourself to me. Otherwise, there is no reason for me to live anymore."

I was looking for a way, a truth, and a life. I was looking everywhere, hungry for something more than the eyes see, reading books about all religions, hoping to touch the truth and fill the void. The country I lived in was still a communist state at the time, and my family was not religious. The only exception was my grandmother.

Sometimes, when I was a child, she would give me a small, shabby book to read. I could not understand what I was reading, but my favorite part was at the end. Whenever I read the last chapters, my heart beat fast with excitement and desire. I cried in my need for somebody who will wipe every tear from my eyes, and for a time when there will be no more death or mourning or crying or pain, for the old order of things has passed away.[1]

In my most desperate time, God found me. In a series of coincidences, divine encounters, and conversations with people who knew Jesus, I heard the gospel for the first time, and experienced a dramatic encounter with God and His love. The truth that I have a heavenly Father who loves me unconditionally, and who will never abuse me and control me, but will support and encourage me till the end, was a fountain of life to me. It pulled me back from the edge of the pit I was about to throw myself into, and gave me meaning and a reason to live. But this was just the beginning.

I have found "the Way, the Truth, and the Life."[2]

The Way is the way of faith. Since the day of my salvation, I've been learning how to live by faith day by day, hour by hour. For me, living by faith means remembering God in my everyday struggles and joys, and doing life together with Him. I train my mind and heart to believe what His Word says, allowing His truths and His Spirit to change me from inside out. When I struggle with guilt, I remember I am forgiven. When the waves of anxiety rise in me, I

---

[1] Revelation 21:4
[2] John 14:6

remember He has given me His peace, and He cares for me. When I am in pain, I remember He is my comforter. I am learning to see a higher reality with my spiritual eyes.

The Truth is that Jesus and I can overcome everything. From the everyday frustrations and worries to life-altering losses and traumas. Through Christ, I have access to God's wisdom and power, and His unlimited resources and provision. He is the way-maker, wave-subduer, miracle-maker, and the lifter of my head. Nothing can separate me from His love. He makes me an overcomer. The more I overcome things with God, things I fear and want to avoid, the more mature I become, and the character of Christ can be fully displayed in me.

The Life is the abundant, eternal life I have been longing for. The eternal life that God offers to everyone through His Son is much greater than any human concept or imagination of self-realization. This is the life every human being is made for—knowing without a doubt who I am, where I belong, where I come from, and where I am going. This is a life of repeated surrender of my desires, plans, dreams, expectations, exchanging them for God's perfect and higher plans and purposes. I am learning to lose control of my ideas of safety, comfort, and predictability, so I can embrace freedom and exceeding joy.

My new life of faith means that every day has a meaning and purpose for me. Even the painful things, my suffering, and tears—nothing is in vain, and everything serves a purpose. All details of my life are part of my transformation and preparation to come home. God is shaping me into a tree of "righteousness, a planting of the Lord for the display of his splendor."[3]

The life of faith is the greatest adventure. When we say yes to God's invitation and decide to take the risk of trusting Him, the adventure begins. Faith is the ticket that allows us

[3] Isaiah 61:3

to participate and find the hidden treasure. Are you ready to embark on it?

LET'S TALK ABOUT FAITH

1. Have you ever felt as if your life was meaningless?

2. Do you know what the purpose of your life is?

3. How could you relate to Hadassah's testimony?

THE GOOD NEWS

Our life has purpose. We were created to be in a relationship with Jesus. To know Him and make Him known.

Chapter 6

Beauty from Ashes

Erika Bailey

I don't recall the details of the moment I accepted Jesus into my heart. I was around twelve years old at our kitchen table with my daddy, an evangelist. I said the sinner's prayer as my dad led me through the Scriptures. I remember getting up from that chair with a smile, a sense of relief, and hugging my daddy. However, if I'm honest, saying the sinner's prayer was what most kids my age did where I grew up.

I was raised in a church pew. Stories about Jesus, and all the stories of old, were instilled in me from my infancy. Becoming "saved" was what you did. Throughout those years, I missed the intimate love that Christ has for me, a true understanding of faith.

Despite the lack, I strived to be faithful to my faith as I grew. Sure, I strayed as a teen and young adult, but I didn't stray as much as my fellow "hell, fire, and brimstone," church pew kids. My husband, Travis and I were married when I was in my early twenties. We wasted no time in starting a family, having two children under the age of three before our third anniversary.

We were in church with our kids every time the doors opened. I read my Bible and a devotion every morning like clockwork, but I usually drifted back to sleep as I read.

> "Behold, to obey is better than sacrifice."
> ~ 1 Samuel 15:22b, NLT

I'd close the Word of God and begin my day with a big check mark off the list of things I needed to do to start my Christian walk off right.

Christianity 101: Read your Bible every morning—*check*.

Sadly, my "time with the Lord" was a to-do list. My heart wasn't in it. Honestly, my whole life was a big Christian to-do list, and I thought I was doing everything right. Even being raised in church and knowing the Bible stories, I never grasped the character of God. I never understood the magnitude of His love for me. I would make sacrifices for Him (go to church, get up early to read His Word, teach Sunday school, etc.), but I failed to be obedient to His calling because my heart wasn't in the right place.

> "Faith shows the reality of what we hope for; it is the evidence of things we cannot see."
> ~ Hebrews 11:1, NLT

Obey comes from the word "Shama" in Greek. It not only means to hear or to hearken, but it can also mean to understand. Faith in the above text means "pistis" in Greek. It means to trust or believe.

How could I wholeheartedly obey God if I didn't truly understand who He was? By not understanding or knowing Him fully, how could I trust Him?

I couldn't.

What I learned is that our loving God will allow us to go to places we never dreamed of in order to understand who He is and His love for us. He allows heartache to posture our hearts towards obedience, which miraculously can renew our faith.

> "Faith shows the reality of what we hope for; it is the evidence of things we cannot see."
> ~ Hebrews 11:1, NLT

That's where I found myself.

Eleven years into my marriage with two children, a great job as a registered nurse working from home, and a beautiful house. God had blessed me beyond belief. Yet I found myself ready to walk away from it all. I wanted to leave my husband for another man I had never met.

Think on that for a minute…

How crazy that very thought is to me, years later as I type it out. It seems completely foolish, and it was. You see, that is exactly how sin works in our lives. Things that seem so foolish in the afterthought are the very things the enemy rationalizes in our minds. As off the wall as it sounds, it can seem perfectly normal when you are in the middle of it.

Confessing to my husband brought a solid marriage to ashes. All that was left was devastation and broken trust. I was shocked at my own demise.

I'd strived for perfection my entire life. Although I knew I was flawed, there were sins I would absolutely turn my nose up at other people for doing. I'd think, "I would *never* do something like that," as though I was exempt from those sins. One of those sins was adultery. So, marking myself with the title "adulterer" was a complete blow to the perfect Christian persona I was striving for.

Consequently, my pride, along with the Christian image I worked so hard to for, took a devastating blow. The destruction of pride was a painful experience for me. Yet looking back, it was the most loving thing God could have given me.

My flesh longed for the destruction of the unity God ordained when my husband and I took our vows. The sinful desires of my flesh were drawn to the act of adultery. However, the Spirit that dwells in me as a believer longs for righteousness. The two are in a constant war with one another.[1] I literally felt that very battle rage inside of me. Still, a decision had to be made.

Having the power of the Holy Spirit in me since my call to Him as a little girl kept me from furthering the utter devastation I'd caused in my marriage. Even though I was not as obedient to Him as I should have been. Even though my life was more of a Christian facade than a life of surrender. Even though my faith was weak, and I didn't even know it. Even though I didn't know God for who He was, despite a lifelong knowledge of Him.

Even though I found myself in this sinful mess, He showed me a truth I'll never forget—I am His.

In that moment, God saved me. Although I believe without a shadow of a doubt God saved me as a little girl at that kitchen table, this experience taught me that the grace of God didn't stop when I got up from that table. The power of Jesus continues to save me from my own foolish ways. He always has, but my pride hindered me from seeing it before. I may not remember the day I said the sinner's prayer, but I will never forget the day God saved me from my own selfish destruction.

That day changed me. It changed my relationship with Him. It humbled me. It allowed me to truly understand and grasp the magnitude of His love. It restored my marriage. It allowed our hearts to soften to His ways, which was a call into foster care, something we would have never considered

---

[1] Galatians 5:16-24

before. Yet despite the pain, shame, and regret of my own sinful choices, God used it for His glory.

I am now a mother of four children: two of my own, and two sisters from foster care. He has given me a ministry and a testimony that I would have never had otherwise. He has given me an unwavering faith by gifting me, with His saving grace time and time again. He is a Savior I can trust. I am living proof that He is a God that restores beauty from ashes.

LET'S TALK ABOUT FAITH

1. How old were you when you accepted Jesus as your Savior?

2. How has God used your sinful choices for His glory?

3. Could you relate to Erika's testimony?

THE GOOD NEWS

Jesus loves us beyond our comprehension, and He will never give up on us.

CHAPTER 7
THE GRACE OF THE GOSPEL

Jamie Kupkovits

> "I waited patiently for the LORD; he turned to me and heard my cry. He lifted me out of the slimy pit, out of the mud and mire; he set my feet on a rock and gave me a firm place to stand. He put a new song in my mouth, a hymn of praise to our God. Many will see and fear the Lord and will put their trust in Him."
> ~ Psalm 40:1-3, NIV

If I close my eyes, I can still see myself there, lying on the floor, tears running down my face like streams of flowing water. My heart ached as my soul cried out in gut-wrenching pain. Everything around me was crumbling. My once comfortable and controlled life became chaotic and anything but certain. The dreams I had envisioned for myself were now indefinitely deferred, and the grief this brought was grueling.

Shattered and shaken, I put my hands up and my head down as I resigned to the fact that it was all gone—the sanctuary I called my home, my idealistic view of family, my finances, and my perceived sense of security. What I'd worked so hard to build and nurture was all gone. I was left with confusion, anxiety and hopelessness—all of which put me into a pit of deep despair.

It was then, in the deepest part of my pit, when a ray of hope and the grace of the gospel shined through the darkness. It was a light that at first shined dimly, but as I learned to listen and follow its holy guidance, my perspective on what was happening to me started to change. The extreme anxiousness I felt turned into a peace that surpassed my chaotic circumstances and limited human understanding. The more I searched for the light, the more the darkness lifted as I realized just how long I'd been blinded by the lies that defined me by what I had and what I did.

I was accustomed to looking down and around me—at what I possessed and what positions I held—to define my worth. But it wasn't until I was on my knees with my head bowed low when I finally looked up to see the Light of Jesus as the hope my weary and broken heart needed.

Jesus spoke to me then, telling me how His heart ached for the pain I felt, and how it hurt Him for me to go through this difficult season. He told me that, in going through tragedy, He'd bring triumph by revealing mysteries that are only learned in the struggle. He'd speak to me, telling me we'd endure every trial together, and in doing so I'd learn to trust Him with every aspect of my life. He'd speak to me by reclaiming deferred dreams and repurposing them to bring about His purposes for my life. He'd speak to me and show me what truly mattered to Him, therefore changing my perspective on life. He'd show me, by losing my worldly comforts, that He is truly all I need.

His holy Word would speak over my worries and give me a faith that stood victorious over my crippling fear. He'd give me a hope that could not be snuffed out when all seemed hopeless. He'd tell me who I am—chosen, accepted, and called. My identity is found in Him and not defined by the ways of this wayward, fleeting world. He came to save me and brought triumph out of tragedy because of His graciousness.

Jesus—my light—changed everything for me. Because of His grace and the message of the gospel, I now stand reclaimed, forgiven, loved, and called to live in the truth of Jesus' promises. I am no longer blinded by the darkness and consumed by lies, because the grace of the gospel gives me a hope that can reach me at any depth, and equips me to keep persevering in the hard times of life.

LET'S TALK ABOUT FAITH

1. Can you remember a moment where you felt like all you had was Jesus?

2. Has Jesus ever spoken to you in your heart?

3. Could you relate to Jamie's testimony?

THE GOOD NEWS

We can't lose the love of Christ. Though everything else may fade away, Jesus stays the same.

CHAPTER 8

DO YOU FEAR GOD?

Jessica Schneider

I recently realized how much fear of God there is in the world. And I don't mean "the-fear-of-God-is-the-beginning-of-knowledge" type of fear. No, I mean flat out fear of God that doesn't lead to knowledge. The type of fear that makes you run away from God, not to Him.

I remember being afraid of God.

I grew up in the church, went through confirmation class at thirteen, got confirmed, and attended church camp. I did not want to go to church camp. I thought it was going to be boring, and I definitely didn't want to spend all day reading the Bible for a week.

I knew about Jesus. I could probably have told you all the stories of His life. I probably passed confirmation class with flying colors, and that was enough for me.

But one year at church camp, there was a Bible study on the Book of Revelation. We couldn't get out of going to Bible studies, just like I couldn't get out of my fear of God.

I thought I knew Him, but I didn't know Him as a best friend. However, what I knew with everything in me was that if I died in that moment, eternal life wasn't waiting for me. Revelation happens once. After we die, we don't get a second chance. And that terrified me.

But over that year, something changed. My fear led me to learn who He really is. I can't say I had a defining moment where I gave my life to Christ. But what I can say is that one day I noticed I didn't hold the same fear of God anymore. My fear turned to gratitude for what He did for me, and my knowing turned personal. I went beyond just knowing stories about Him. I knew He was my Savior.

No longer was I terrified of Revelation, but in awe of the beauty that waits for those who believe in God's only Son, Jesus. I mean… Revelation 21:4 is a beautiful promise.

> "He will wipe every tear from their eyes. There will be no more death, or mourning or crying or pain."
> ~ Psalm 40:1-3, NIV

And I can confidently say He rescued me. He is my strong tower. He has never abandoned me. He walked with me through the storm. He gave me peace in the chaos. He has been faithful even when I have been faithless.

He is *my* God.

Have you ever stopped to consider all of this? The fear of God? Faith? Knowing about Him, verses *knowing* Him?

Recently, a loved one was dying. He knew he was dying, and I wondered what that feels like. Was he afraid? Was he ready? Did he wish it would come faster? Or did he ask for more time? Was he at peace, or was he wrestling with his salvation, and if he had "done enough" to get to heaven? I don't know, but for me, these were very sobering thoughts.

I love how Jesus responds to us in our time of need, when we reach out to Him in faith. This is displayed beautifully in Scripture. In John 5, Jesus found a man waiting by the pool to be healed, but no one ever came to help him. He was paralyzed and had been waiting for healing for thirty-eight years.

Jesus heard of his condition and asked him if he wanted to be well. The man replied, "I have no one to help me into the pool when the water is stirred. While I am trying to get in, someone else goes down ahead of me."[1]

So basically, he said "yes, I want to be healed, but…" Honestly, his situation probably looked pretty hopeless. Jesus responded by saying, "Take up your mat and walk." Jesus spoke, and the man did as Jesus said.[2]

Like this man, sometimes our situation seems hopeless too, especially when we are facing certain death. But the story of the paralyzed man shows us that when you trust He is God, you see that He is God.

This takes me to another man in Scripture. He was also faced certain death. There was no hope for him to survive. Death was a sure thing. A miracle wasn't going to happen here. Not this time.

It happened as Jesus hung on the cross. There were two other men hanging on crosses beside Him. All three of their deaths were certain. One mocked Jesus, saying, "Aren't you the Messiah? Save yourself, and us."

The other responded, "Don't you fear God?" This man knew they were being punished justly. He also knew that Jesus didn't deserve this death sentence.

Knowing everything he had done and what he deserved, the man made one request: "Jesus, remember me when you come into your kingdom."

The man acknowledged who Jesus was, and Jesus responded to his faith by saying, "Truly, truly today you will be with me in paradise."

---

[1] John 5:7
[2] John 5:8

This man's fear of God led him to a faith that secured his salvation.

So how do we move from fearing God to deeply knowing who He is, despite our circumstances?

One way is to trust Him. We believe He is who He says He is, and then we walk when He says walk, even amid our excuses and "buts."

Another way is to approach Him in full faith and ask Him to remember us in His kingdom, trusting that when you get to paradise, He will be waiting with a place prepared just for you.

LET'S TALK ABOUT FAITH

1. Do you understand the fear of the Lord?

2. Do you believe God is who He says He is? Share who He is in your own words.

3. Could you relate to Jessica's testimony?

THE GOOD NEWS

Jesus is God the Son, sent to earth to live a perfect life and die a sinner's death because of God's great love for us—for me. He loved me so much He died for me.

CHAPTER 9

WITH MY WHOLE HEART

Pamela A. Taylor

> "For I know the thoughts I think toward you, says the LORD, thoughts of peace and not of evil, to give you a future and a hope. Then you will call upon Me and go and pray to Me, and I will listen to you. And you will seek Me and find Me, when you search for Me with your heart."
> ~ Jeremiah 29:11-13, NKJV

I grew up in the days when you didn't talk about religion or politics. And you especially didn't talk about feelings. You just lived out the life you'd been "dealt" without question or complaint. There were few time-saving appliances, so our priority was just living life.

My mother was in and out of the hospital most of my young life, and she died when I was twelve. I remember how everyone adored her and flocked to her bedside in what had once been our living room. I, too, adored her. There was something different about her.

I remember one day my father sent me upstairs to make the beds. The family doctor was making a house call. I remember getting on my knees and sobbing beside the bed my mom and dad shared before she'd become bedridden and moved downstairs. After I told God (whom I did not know) that I couldn't stand seeing her that way, I felt immediate peace and calm.

Then my father called for me to come downstairs. The doctor had left. My mother had died. And, in my young mind, my "prayer" to my unknown God had killed her.

Then, my boyfriend and I had a huge fight, so instead of spending the day with me, he went water skiing. Later that day, I got a phone call from a classmate. My boyfriend fell while skiing and was run over by a boat driven by another classmate. His entire midsection was hit by the motor blades. No one could survive that. I blamed our fight. I thought his death was my fault.

My best friend left for a family vacation and was gone the entire summer. I felt empty inside. I was lonely and lost, but no one talked about their feelings in those days. I spent my summer walking back and forth from my house, past that dreaded lake, to the cemetery. While there, I talked to the tombstones of my mom and my boyfriend. "Why did you leave me? I *need* you!!!" Lots of tears watered both graves all summer long.

In the fall, I began my new life without a mother. I came home from school every day and started dinner. My dad was an insurance salesman, so he was in and out of the house. It was very good to have him always checking in and so available. I was a "good" kid. I did the ironing while my brother and I fought over which TV program to watch.

About four years later, I graduated from high school and went off to college as expected. I got good grades, but it was awful at college. My small-town innocence met the college decadence of the 1960s. One Friday the thirteenth, I went on a blind date. He was in the army, so he soon left for his overseas assignment. He called often in the middle of the night (which was his daytime). When he came home, we got married. He worked as a traveling salesman, so he was only home on the weekends.

I had some really great jobs. Things seemed great for me, but a weekend marriage is tough. I was successful and occupied with my work, and so was he. We were living with no thought of God. I don't think God even entered our mind during those days.

After many moves to different states, always living far from my family and childhood friends, I quit working outside the home to work on my marriage. I wanted to be a "good wife." That was the days of *The Total Woman* book movement. Instead of just existing, I started to think "what if…?" What if I was a "good wife?" Would my husband love me then? We saw a marriage counselor, but that was a disaster!

Then, one evening, I noticed the church ads in the Sunday paper. I thought, "Maybe I will try church." My only criteria were: It must be close by, and it must have a service later that evening. The church down the street from us qualified.

I had been searching for something my whole life. Maybe this was at least part of my answer? My mom had something different when she was alive. Most church people seemed to have the same thing my mom had. I wanted it! But what was it?

I found it there at that little church down the street. The pastor was a true shepherd. He loved his flock. The people welcomed me, loved me, nurtured me, and discipled me. I was a broken, lonely failure. I was twenty-seven years old. On June 1st, 1975, *with my whole heart*, I committed my life to Jesus Christ and was baptized by immersion. On that day, I put my hand to the plow and have not looked back!

I am in love with Jesus because He first loved me. Before I even knew Him, He came to die for my sins. For your sins. He died on that cross for me and for you. He rose from the dead, went to prepare a place for you and for me, and He is coming back again! Yay! Can you believe it? It is true!

Another truth is that Jesus directed my life to search for the something special my mother had. And when I realized I'd needed Him all along, He showed me where to find Him. My new church family became "Jesus with skin on," and they loved me with all my scars and flaws. I'd finally found what my heart had searched for my whole life.

Once I was blind and now, I see. And I spend my days writing and coaching and talking about my first love, the Lord Jesus Christ. He loves me with His whole heart. His love makes me free to love Him back with my whole heart.

LET'S TALK ABOUT FAITH

1. Have you ever known someone who had that "something" Pam saw? Where you could tell just by being around them that something was different?

2. Who has impacted your faith?

3. How could you relate to Pam's testimony?

THE GOOD NEWS

When we look for God, we will find Him. God doesn't sit in heaven far away and look down on us from above. He is right here with us.

CHAPTER 10

WHAT IS THAT SOMETHING?

Heather Hart

My mom wrote about it in chapter one, and Pam shared about it in the last chapter, but what is it? What is the something the Bible and some Christians have that no one else seems to? What do others see in us?

It isn't an "it" as much as it is a person. It's the Holy Spirit.

Here are a few verses from the Bible that talk about Him:

1. John 14:16, NIV - "And I (Jesus) will ask the Father, and he will give you another advocate to help you and be with you forever."
2. Acts 2:38, NIV - "Repent and be baptized, every one of you, in the name of Jesus Christ for the forgiveness of your sins. And you will receive the gift of the Holy Spirit."
3. 2 Corinthians 3:17, NIV - "Now the Lord is the Spirit, and where the Spirit of the Lord is, there is freedom."

4. Romans 15:13, NIV - "May the God of hope fill you with all joy and peace as you trust in him, so that you may overflow with hope by the power of the Holy Spirit."

5. Romans 5:5, NIV - "And hope does not put us to shame, because God's love has been poured out into our hearts through the Holy Spirit, who has been given to us."

Freedom. Love. Joy. Peace. These are all evidence of the Holy Spirit living in us.

When we accept Jesus as our Savoir, the Holy Spirit comes to live inside us and changes us from the inside out. That doesn't mean we are instantly perfect (we're not), but we are no longer living alone. We have the very Spirit of God with us every moment of every day. And it shows. People can see Him shining out of us. Even if they don't recognize who He is or what they're seeing.

LET'S TALK ABOUT FAITH

1. Have you given much thought to the Holy Spirit—the Spirit of God—living inside of you?

2. Can you look back and see the work of the Holy Spirit in your life?

3. Do you think others can see the Holy Spirit living in you?

THE GOOD NEWS

Jesus sent His advocate, the Holy Spirit, to live inside those of us who belong to Him. That means we are never alone, and no matter what life throws our way, Jesus is always right there with us.

CHAPTER 11

A VERY PRECIOUS FRIENDSHIP

Esther Florence

It was a beautiful day, and a wonderful couple were expecting their third baby. Everyone said it would be a boy since they already had two girls, but it was a pretty little girl—me! Living in India, the successive girl child is not considered very auspicious because of all the costs attached, especially the dowry. However, my dad was different. He loved the Lord Jesus and believed that children are the Lord's heritage, so he distributed sweets to celebrate my birth.

I grew up with strong Christian values. We had family prayer daily, and we attended both church and Sunday school regularly. Dad was a respected officer in the Indian customs, and despite all the corruption, he was a very honest officer. We loved and served the Lord Jesus as a family.

At the age of ten, while attending a vacation Bible school in Delhi, India, I accepted the Lord Jesus after I heard the story of Ti-Pham, a young girl from Africa. There my journey with the Lord Jesus began. I fell in love with my Bible and it has been my favorite book ever since. I would read ten to fifteen chapters together and spend a long time in prayer, even at a very young age.

> "There is a friend who sticks closer than a brother."
> ~ Proverbs 18:24, KJV

Christ had become very personal to me. He was the friend to whom I would share my fears, my doubts, my anxieties, and all my heart. He would clearly speak to me through His Word. I would share the Lord Jesus with my friends.

Towards the end of that same year, my sister was talking about the second coming of Jesus. I was not sure there would be a place for me in heaven, so I prayed, "Lord, please give me the assurance that if I die, I will go to heaven."

A few days later, I read Ezekiel 36:26-27 during a church sermon. The passage is written in future tense as the Lord promises, "I will give you a new heart," and "I will put my Spirit in you." But as I read it, I heard the Lord speak to me in past tense, that He had already given me a new heart and a new spirit. Then I was sure the Lord had forgiven all my sins. I knew He was with me and He had given me a new life in Him.

As I grew, so did an inferiority complex and exceptionally low self-esteem. I felt I was of no worth, and not as beautiful or talented as other girls. Then a counselor at a Bible camp for teens assured me I was precious. She said, "No matter how useless or worthless people may say you are, the Lord Jesus has created you for a purpose and you are very precious to Him." I held on to that. My friend, Jesus, is by my side always, so why worry what the world says?

I completed my education, found a good job, and got married. The Lord was by my side at each stage. He led me through and helped me to do His will in my life.

I experienced the miraculous hand of the Lord during the birth of my first child. My feet and face were quite swollen. A visit to the doctor confirmed that my blood pressure was so high that I had to be admitted to the hospital immediately. I thought my blood pressure would go down so I could go home, but after a few days, it remained high.

On the morning of March 24th, still thinking that I would be discharged soon, I heard a loud voice clearly say, "Nothing is impossible with God." About an hour later, the doctor said they had to do surgery immediately because the baby's heartbeat was slowing down. I had only one prayer: "Lord, I want a normal, healthy baby." Later that evening, by the grace of God, I delivered a baby girl. She weighed just 3.3 pounds, so they moved her to another hospital's neonatal ICU before I could even see her. I was afraid, but knowing she was alive gave me peace. All was well, because the Lord Jesus was with me, and He is mighty and strong. My precious baby is a healthy God-fearing teen today. Truly, the Lord is faithful.

Shortly after the Lord blessed me with another baby girl, we had to face a difficult situation in our married life. My husband resigned from his job because he was wrongly accused of misconduct. We had two young girls and no other source of income. That Sunday in church, a brother sang a special song about a dialogue between a child and a sparrow.

The song brought me to tears and gave me the calm assurance that the Lord would take care of us.

My husband found a new job in a few months, but it was so stressful that he quit. I had been away from the workplace for almost six years, but I got a job with a reputable firm later that evening. I quickly found a babysitter so my husband could look for work. It took nearly six months, but eventually he also found a good job, so the Lord blessed us

> "Are not two sparrows sold for a cent? And yet not one of them will fall to the ground apart from your Father. But the very hairs of your head are all numbered. So do not fear; you are more valuable than many sparrows."
> ~ Matthew 10:29-31, NASB

both in our work. Every day, like any other working mom, I have struggles, heartaches, and joys. However, I have a precious Friend who never lets me go, who walks with me through the valleys and the mountains.

From a very young age, the fear of death of a loved one haunted me. In September 2005, the Lord suddenly called my father-in-law home, and then in September 2020, my dad was called to glory. Death is truly very painful, but Psalm 23:4a says "Yea though I walk through the valley of the shadow of death, I will fear no evil." The blessed hope we have in the Lord Jesus that we will meet our loved ones again keeps me going. To experience loss is truly tough, especially when I see an empty chair, or miss a loving voice. But I remember my friend, the Lord Jesus, is real. He comforts with His presence and the calm assurance that there is hope beyond the grave.

Each day is precious with the Lord by my side. I speak to Him as a friend, and He speaks to me from His Word. I have nothing to fear as long as I rest my faith in Him. My best friend, Jesus, is very precious. If you haven't experienced this personal relationship with Him, give it a try. You will never be disappointed.

> "O death, where is thy sting,
> O grave where is thy victory."
> ~ 1 Corinthians 15:55, KJV

LET'S TALK ABOUT FAITH

1. Are you afraid of death?

2. Have you ever felt unworthy?

3. How else could you relate to Esther's testimony?

THE GOOD NEWS

We were created by a God who loves us more than we could ever imagine, and our worth comes from Him.

CHAPTER 12

ALWAYS THERE

Lyssa Williams

For a long time, I only knew of God, but did not know Him for myself.

The familiarity of hearing godly words and attending church services from birth drowned out the simple yet powerful truth of the gospel; the fact that Jesus loves me and died for me.

As I grew older, I developed an anxiety disorder as a result of a dysfunctional home. As time passed, I strayed from what I learned about Jesus. Mental health seemed to be in the total opposite direction from religion, and this consumed my life. The harder I struggled with anxiety, the more I felt further away from God. The feelings of distance that I felt between God and I were not true, however. God was still with me, even through anxiety, beckoning me to His love and showering me with His unconditional love, even when I questioned His presence.

I can distinctly recall asking my mother one day, why should I choose God just to not go to hell. My thoughts were, why should I serve a god out of fear? Boy, was I mistaken about having a relationship with Jesus. Some months after having that conversation with my mother, Jesus found me smack in the middle of anxiety, questions, and doubts.

For some time, I had been listening to worship music that my older sister suggested to me. I was drawn to the singer's love and passion for God; the songs were love songs to God. I did not know it then, but those songs were planting seeds in me. I wanted to feel the love and passion for God too, just like the singer. I felt like God was speaking to me through those songs, saying come home, there is more for me. I could not believe He still wanted to give me a chance after years of not talking to Him, running away from Him, and not believing in Him as I should have. His mercy and grace covered all my shortcomings.

About two months after I started listening to the songs, I decided to say a prayer asking Jesus to come into my life. If Jesus was willing to still find me despite years of running from Him, then I wanted to really give Him a try. Nervously, I eventually made the decision to get baptized some weeks after saying the prayer. After being baptized, I still struggled with anxiety and knowing who God is, and who I am in Him. I had so many questions about what was next in my relationship with Him. I know I came across a Christian book during this time, in it said that when a person gets baptized, it is not a one-time thing; the Holy Spirit is constantly doing a new work in your life, like a continual baptism. I breathed a

> "Your unfailing love, O LORD, is as vast as the heavens; your faithfulness reaches beyond the clouds. Your righteousness is like the mighty mountains, Your justice like the ocean depths. You care for people and animals alike, O LORD. How precious is Your unfailing love, O God! All humanity finds shelter in the shadow of Your wings."
> ~ Psalm 36:5-7, NLT

sigh of relief after reading this. I felt so happy on the inside knowing that my one act of saying yes to being baptized meant God would do the hard work of changing me, I just had to be a willing vessel. I was once a skeptic, but God's unconditional love pushed past my lack of understanding and sins, where He found me. God's love was the love I never knew I needed.

Not only is God's Spirit constantly changing me for the better, but I now also experience His divine love which comforts and reassures me through anxious moments in a way that no person ever could. The more I allow God into my battles with anxiety, is the more I see that mental health and religion aren't opposites. The God who made my mind, knows best how it should function. The light of His truth gives me peace that all is well.

I have learned that having questions is not a deterrent to God. He knows we will have questions, and He is there to give us answers and peace about whatever may be hard for us to understand.

As God's child, I now have a boldness that is rooted in the promises found in His Word. It blows my mind that I am now a new being all because of the power of the gospel of Christ.

As a wife and mother, it goes without saying, that I love my family. But that love couldn't be possible without God; after all, God is love. We are all expressions of His love. The same love that made the cross and the gospel of Christ possible. More than that, God loves us way more than our family ever would; I still cannot fully fathom that truth right now.

Life may not be perfect, but I know for sure that I am forever changed by God's love; a love that was always there.

> "I will be glad and rejoice in Your unfailing love, for You have seen my troubles, and You care about the anguish of my soul."
>
> ~ Psalm 31:7, NLT

LET'S TALK ABOUT FAITH

1. Could you relate to Lyssa's testimony?

2. Do you consider yourself a child of God? How does that truth affect your life?

3. How has God's love affected your life?

THE GOOD NEWS

We can never run too far from Jesus. He is always there, loving us, and ready to start (or continue) a relationship with us.

Part Two

Walking the Talk

CHAPTER 13

CHRISTIAN WOMEN & THE GOSPEL

Heather Hart

The day started off fairly normal. I spent some time with Jesus, got my kids ready for school, came home and ate breakfast. I even postponed going straight to my desk in favor of some extended quiet time. Then I buckled down and got to work. That's when Satan stepped in, and things quickly spiraled out of control.

Have you ever been so upset you were physically shaking? That's where I was that morning. It seemed like everything I touched was falling to pieces (literally). In hindsight, it could have been worse, but in the moment, I was done.

I may have actually looked at my Bible with scorn as I wondered how the gospel could fix this. Thankfully, God came through (He always does). After a few tears, I picked up my Bible and started to read. I lost myself in an Old Testament story. It didn't speak to the moment at hand, but it took my eyes off my problems and put them back on Jesus. *And that is exactly what I needed.*

A little while later I looked up Psalm 62:2. I had been trying to memorize it, and I think Satan must have taken it as a challenge. It says, "[God] alone is my rock and my salvation, my fortress, I shall not be greatly shaken."

I had most definitely been greatly shaken. I felt like a failure. In my moment of distress, I didn't look to Jesus. I didn't cling to the cross. I let Satan win.

But God…

We all need a good "but God" moment now and again, don't we? Well, I felt like a failure, but God whispered in my heart with words I will never forget. *"You didn't fail. You slipped and fell. Now let Me help you up so we can try again."* If you've ever been there, take a moment to let those words sink in.

You are not a failure.

I love God's foresight. Earlier that morning, I read a devotional by Angela Nazworth. She wrote about days she spent at the skating rink as a teen, even though she didn't really know how to skate. She clung to the carpet wall, afraid to fall. She wrote about how fear held her hostage. It kept her from embracing all that the skating rink had to offer. [1]

She wrote about a girl with big hair who skated with ease, but still fell now and again. The difference was that when the big hair girl fell, she got back up. She didn't let it keep her down. She didn't call it quits. She just stood back up and started going again.

That's where God found me that day. I had fallen, and I needed to get back up. Jesus had His hand stretched out, and I needed to grab hold.

Living In Light of the Gospel

---

[1] The (in)courage Community *Craving Connection* (Nashville, TN: B&H Publishing Group, 2017), pp. 16.

Years ago, I was introduced to the idea that the gospel wasn't just for the unsaved. It wasn't a one-time thing, but an everyday thing. The love and forgiveness of Christ isn't something that we ever stop needing. Here's what happened…

The pastor's wife at my church was leading us through a study on women counseling women. Our homework assignment was to read the book *Counsel from the Cross* by Elyse Fitzpatrick and Dennis Johnson. In it, Elyse wrote, "We don't need a self-help book, we need a Savior. We don't need to get our collective act together; we need death and resurrection and the life-transforming truths of the gospel. And we don't need them just once, at the beginning of our Christian life, we need them every moment of every day."[2]

Think about the magnitude of that for a minute.

Jesus isn't just someone who lived and died, He lived and died *for us*. He rose again, ascended into heaven *for us*. He sent His Spirit to live in the hearts of all who believe in Him with the promise of life everlasting in the presence of God—*that's us*. And it changes everything.

A few years ago, I met a wonderful woman. We went to the same church and Bible study, and our children often played together, but we weren't inseparable. We never shared our pasts or any tears, but her words left a memorable impact on my life. Here's what she said: "I've got a lot of baggage in my past. When I came here, I was pretty screwed up. But God brought me through it, and I am through it. If it bothers people, that's between them and God, because it doesn't bother me anymore."

I absolutely love the peace she has about her past mistakes. I don't know her story or how grievous her sin was, but I know it happened while she was a believer, not

---

[2] Elyse M. Fitzpatrick and Dennis E. Johnson, in *Counsel from the Cross: Connecting Broken People to the Love of Christ* (Wheaton, IL: Crossway Books, 2009), pp. 30

before. Christians aren't insta-perfect. We still make mistakes, and God brings us through them.

In fact, the only real difference between Christians and non-Christians isn't about us at all. It lies in the gospel. We have accepted that we will never and can never be perfect. We know we need the perfect blood of Christ to grant us forgiveness, not only for the mistakes of our past, but for the mistakes we make each and every day. The gospel is just as important for Christians as it is for non-Christians. The only difference is that we are supposed to recognize the power in the blood of Christ.

That is my prayer—that I don't take the gospel for granted. Not when it comes to my sin, and not when it comes to the sin of others. God sent His Son, part of Himself, to die so that we could be forgiven of our numerous, horrific sins—all of them. He is so amazing, isn't He?

But how does that change our lives? Why does the gospel matter in the everyday, nitty-gritty, mundane moments? That's what we are going to discuss in the following chapters as a dozen different women share how God impacts their lives each day. They talk about everything from the way they view church attendance to parenting their children. From working outside the home to studying the Bible. These are women just like you who have made Jesus part of their everyday lives.

LET'S TALK ABOUT FAITH

1. When things get rough, where do you turn?

2. When others are upset with you, do you internalize it, or recognize when it's their problem and not yours?

3. Can you think of a way the gospel impacts your life on a regular basis?

THE GOSPEL FOR TODAY

Even when we fall short or mess up, God's love and forgiveness never fails.

CHAPTER 14

OUR FAITHFUL DEFENDER

Valerie Riese

> "The Lord is my strength and my shield; my heart trusts
> in him, and he helps me. My heart leaps for joy, and
> with my song I praise him."
> ~ Psalm 28:7, NIV

"What scares you the most?" My husband's question fractured the silence as we drove to the hospital.

Oblivious to my surroundings, I contemplated his question. There was so much to be afraid of: surgery, chemotherapy, radiation, side effects... After three days, saying the "c" word (cancer) still made me nauseous.

We emerged from underneath the overpass and the hospital campus came into view, taking me back to the last time we drove in heavy silence to this place.

A few years prior, I struggled with a rare, incurable brain disease called pseudotumor cerebri. I was three years into an untreatable migraine, narrowing vision, and splintered brain function the day my husband appointed our eight-year-old daughter to look after me while he spoke with a computer salesperson. When my little girl transitioned into her parental role without question, I knew I was of no use to anyone anymore.

Panic attacks and fear of debilitating pain, along with eventual blindness and dependency, pushed me to a breaking point. I didn't want to die; I was just too afraid to live anymore. Concerned for my safety, my husband consented to my pleas and took me to the hospital, where I stayed for nearly a week.

The disease went into remission, but the panic attacks continued until I learned to control my anxiety through medication and by leaning on Jesus through scripture and prayer. Now, as we pulled into the parking lot, I knew what part of breast cancer scared me the most—the fear.

The cancer team had mostly good news. The annual mammogram caught the cancer early, so chemotherapy wasn't necessary. Unfortunately, the standard medication prescribed to prevent a recurrence of estrogen fed cancer in premenopausal women is known to cause pseudotumor cerebri. At forty-four, I had a lot of time for cancer to come back.

Without the medication, there were two options: suppress the estrogen by forcing my body into early menopause or decline preventive treatment and hope for the best.

The doctors explained that each option came with risks, but neither one was wrong in my situation. I had to decide between sudden, early menopause or live with an elevated risk of getting cancer again.

It boiled down to fear.

But first I had to beat cancer before deciding how to prevent it from coming back. And there was plenty of fear to fight in the meantime.

The day before my lumpectomy, my husband asked me the same question: "What part do you dread the most?" I imagined entering the operating room without the man who always had enough strength for both of us and said: "What I dread the most is the moment you can't be with me anymore."

The next day, my stomach jumped when my husband had to let go of my hand. With my hand still open, I silently prayed, "Jesus, I'm afraid. Please come with me. Please hold my hand." Warmth suddenly filled the void in my palm and forced out an exhale as my body relaxed. The surgery was over in no time.

Then came radiation. The lingering smell of disinfectant led the way to a round, dimly lit room where the giant radiation machine waited. The technician positioned my exposed body on a cold table extending from the machine.

The sound of approaching footsteps signaled yet another unfamiliar face would appear above me to measure my positioning to prepare for the first treatment. I lifted my head and saw someone approaching, but without my glasses, all I could see was dark blue smocks.

I let my head rest, but without warning, a man appeared and stared at my chest! When I gasped, he looked up and saw the horror and violation in my pale face. He held up what looked like a pen and explained, "I'm sorry. I just need to make a quick pen-tip tattoo right in the center of your chest to guide the radiation rays." He reached over as tears trickled down to the starchy sheet.

Another silent drive home until my husband looked at me with bloodshot eyes and stuttered, "You look traumatized."

Every day I lay there half naked while the staff observed from an adjacent control room. Each time the machine stopped rotating, I pushed out my lungs and held my breath to create a vacuum designed to minimize the radiation exposure to my heart and lungs. To hold my breath as long as possible, I cautiously studied a menacing, bright red light piercing through a large hole in the ceiling until the technician permitted me to breathe again.

But there was another presence with me. As the machine hummed, and the table twitched beneath me, I closed my eyes and called on my comforter: "I trust you, Jesus. Thank you for making me brave. Please help me trust you more." The warmth of His presence in the palm of my open hand whisked me away to a peaceful place of quiet waters where He comforted my soul.

Fatigue and burns gave way to fear and dread as daily treatments continued. I listened to music on the way to treatments for comfort. My favorite song was "My Defender" by Jeremy Camp. I sang along at the top of my lungs, declaring to the fear that Jesus was all I needed, He is my defender. As I sang, the fear faded so I could walk into the cancer center with a measure of confidence.

One night I fell asleep agonizing about my chances of a recurrence. In a dream, I sat terrified in a field, curled up with my knees to my chest as the blackest darkness closed in. Jesus stood between me and the darkness. He spread His arms, creating a barrier the fear could not cross. As the darkness retreated, rays of light revealed that I was peacefully sound asleep in the shadow of a cross as Jesus stood in front of me with His arms spread wide.

Upon awakening, I realized I don't have to fight anxiety. Jesus wants to do it for me. All I have to do is surrender my fears at the cross, trust Him, and rest in the faith that the sacrifice of His blood was enough.

A few months later, a nurse handed me a blue folder of survivor's pamphlets, shook my hand and said "Congratulations, you are cancer-free! When is your appointment with the oncologist to discuss prevention options?"

"I'm not meeting with the oncologist," I told her. "I'll be fine no matter what happens."

Please know that I don't advocate declining treatment in expectation of a miracle. I made my decision with my cancer team. But I did not make my decision based on fear.

So how am I dealing with the uncertainty of a recurrence?

I have more peace than I've had in decades.

Jesus revealed His faithfulness and healed my anxiety through breast cancer, but He isn't a genie in a bottle writing one-and-done, feel-good stories. Jesus is about relationships. He gives me His peace beyond understanding every day through a lifestyle of Scripture, prayer, music, and writing. He is my comforter, my defender, and He never leaves me.

Jesus wants a relationship with you, too. He wants you to surrender your fear for His promises, but He loves you too much to manipulate or control you into obedience.

Instead, He died on earth so you could live with Him in heaven. So surrender your fears to Jesus because He first surrendered His life for you. Then you too can abide in peaceful surrender to your faithful Defender.

3 SCRIPTURES TO EMBRACE WHEN LIFE IS SCARY

1. For I, the Lord your God, will hold your right hand, Saying to you, 'Fear not, I will help you.' (Isaiah 41:13).
2. This is the confidence we have in approaching God: that if we ask anything according to his will, he hears us (1 John 5:14).
3. Cast all your anxiety on him because he cares for you (1 Peter 5:7).

LET'S TALK ABOUT FAITH

1. Have you ever been in a situation you knew was out of your control?

2. How do you handle fear?

3. Do you have a Scripture you can cling to when life spins out of control?

4. Could you relate to Valerie's testimony?

THE GOSPEL FOR TODAY

No matter how out of control my life is, God is with me.

CHAPTER 15

PRACTICAL FAITH

Sarah J Callen

Are you ever amazed at how much your world can change over just a few short months? That's how I feel when I look back at 2020. Though we're only a few months removed from the year, I'm not sure I'll ever be the same.

I've been a Christian for nearly half my life. I first met the Lord when I was sixteen and have been following Him ever since. He has completely changed my life, and I can say with certainty that I would not be where I am today without Him.

Though I've worked at churches and Christian organizations over the years, it has always been easy for me to fall into a comfortable level of Christianity. It's the version of following God where you're nice to people, go to church on Sundays, give sometimes, and do your Christian activities that don't really upset anyone. Though I was following God, I was doing it on my timetable, in my comfort zone, and in my way. I wanted to meet with God and have a relationship with Him, but I wanted it all to be on my terms.

Of course, that's not at all how Jesus operates.

In 2020, I hit a wall of sorts. I realized I had been living off second-hand revelation. Though I loved the Lord, I wasn't following Him as I should have been. I wasn't fully devoted to Him and His ways, though I'm not sure anyone else would've noticed. So, I began to read the Bible for myself again, sometimes reading an entire book of the Bible in one day. I devoured the Word and craved hearing God's voice. I was learning so much about Him!

When I made my way into the Book of Luke, I was really convicted by the chasm between how Jesus lived and how I live. I was struck by how much I value comfort and how little Jesus regarded His own body. I realized how quickly I defend myself when Jesus didn't say a word as He was betrayed and unjustly beaten, mocked, and killed. My priorities didn't match up with how Jesus lived while He was here on earth.

As I engaged with the Word of God, I realized there were certain passages I believed with my whole heart and others I labeled as "nice to have," or as a suggestion. I had no problem believing that God made the world, animals, plants, humans, and more with the power of His words. I was convinced that Jesus performed all the incredible healings recorded in the Bible. I could picture Him turning water into wine, casting out demons, and setting people free. I believed that the Holy Spirit led Paul strategically as he spread the gospel throughout the early church.

But there were other verses I didn't apply in my life. These passages are just as holy as those I walked in, but I didn't value them as highly. I didn't want to give them much of my time because they required me to change how I lived. Like when Jesus said in Matthew 25 that however His followers treated the hungry, thirsty, and sick was how they (we) treated Him. Or that we are to "Do nothing from selfish ambition or conceit, but in humility count others more significant than yourselves."[1]

As God began uncovering these things in me, my only response was to stop and repent. I had to turn from my ways and my value system and ask God to help me adopt His.

I really wish I could say that one prayer of repentance magically reoriented my entire life, but it was merely the start of the journey. I feel like I'm doing that "walking out" of my salvation that Paul writes about in Philippians 2:12. For years, I coasted on autopilot, doing the culturally approved Christian activities. I simply can't coast by any longer.

Now, when I read the Bible, especially the words and works of Jesus, I feel so convicted. I used to feel good or encouraged by many of Jesus' sermons, but now I realize the extent of my own desire for the pleasures of this world. I realize how much my longing for comfort contradicts what Jesus said. And how my wants often fly in the face of the kingdom of God.

Though I have been a Christian for many years, I am living my faith in a more practical and tangible way than I was before. The restorative work of Jesus' life is becoming more evident in how I speak to others, the causes I donate to, how I spend my time, and so much more. I'm no longer content to just slap a "Jesus" sticker on my life and still live like the world. I really want to live like Jesus, even though I know that means daily dying to myself and my own desires.

Thankfully, Jesus is multifaceted, and He can be more than one thing at a time. Even though I feel challenged and convicted by His Word, I'm also comforted by His presence. Knowing the character of God fills me with hope.

It's impossible to follow the words and ways of Jesus in our own strength. Thankfully, we're not expected to muscle through life by our own willpower. God has given us

---

[1] Philippians 2:3

Himself, His Word, and His people to lead us through life. I think I'm more aware of my weakness and shortcomings in this season than I have been in the past, but I'm also more aware of God's goodness and ever-present grace in my life.

I'm grateful that I have disengaged autopilot and handed over the wheel to Jesus. He's changing me, which radically changes the way I live my life. The Bible is no longer a religious text that I read to check off a box. It is a practical guide to daily living. My faith has moved from a theoretical or religious arena and is affecting every area of my life.

I feel like Paul when he wrote, "One thing I do: forgetting what lies behind and straining forward to what lies ahead, I press on toward the goal for the prize of the upward call of God in Christ Jesus."[2]

Through the empowerment of the Holy Spirit living within us, let's look forward and move toward God. Let's courageously answer His call and choose to die to ourselves daily, just as Christ did for us.

LET'S TALK ABOUT FAITH

1. Do you ever feel like you're living on autopilot?

2. Sarah called us to look forward and move toward God. How can remembering the gospel every day help us do just that?

3. How else could you relate to Sarah's testimony?

---

[2] Philippians 3:13b-14

THE GOSPEL FOR TODAY

I want to live like Jesus, but even when I fail, I'm covered by the blood of Christ and there is no condemnation because I belong to Him.

CHAPTER 16
THE DIVINE EXCHANGE

Dr. Karen Michelle Ricci

Turn your eyes upon Jesus
Look full in His wonderful face
And the things of earth will grow strangely dim
In the light of His glory and grace.
Helen Howarth Lemmel[1]

Like many people, when thinking of my childhood, a myriad of complex emotions rises within me. Happy memories mingle with themes of neglect, feeling horribly misunderstood and often overlooked, themes which followed me well into adulthood.

I thought being a child who not only internalized everything but also felt so deeply about so much worked against me. Being told that I was "too sensitive" or even "silly" because I expressed an emotion was very common, always hurtful, and never helped. However, feeling deeply is also what helped draw me to my first love, Jesus.

---

[1] Howarth, Helen. "Turn Your Eyes Upon Jesus." 1922.

When I was three years old, a relative asked if I loved him and I replied, "No, I love Jesus." He then asked if I loved him after my love for Jesus, and I replied, "No, I love Coke." My priorities as a young child were pretty hilarious! That "love" for Coca-Cola remained strong for years afterward, but at least my love for Jesus came first!

My earliest memories of Jesus come from songs. "Jesus Loves Me" was the first song I can remember singing in church, around the age of two... and I believed it! "Jesus Loves the Little Children" was another song I remember learning during my toddler years that all children were precious to Jesus, no matter what culture or race.

These songs and others are treasures deeply imprinted on my heart. The Jesus I knew was loving, kind, and the most wonderful person you'd ever meet. In my young spirit, I'd imagine running up to Jesus and climbing in His lap for a hug. These truths were real, and life was simple. He loved me and all the children of the world!

As I got older, life became complicated. In my personal experience as a former pastor's child, home life and church life were rarely separate. Both worlds placed heaps of external expectations upon me while simultaneously ignoring my internal needs.

However, as the difficulties of life grew, so did my internal song list. My prayers were often in the form of songs. My heart became a spiritual jukebox, of sorts, filled with songs that I could pull out anytime and sing along with. As I grew in spirit, a shift occurred where not only was I singing about Jesus but was also singing to Him.

Whenever I felt sad, I would sing to Him. Whenever I felt angry, I'd sing to Him. Whenever I was in pain, I'd sing to Him. If I made a mistake, I would sing to Him. Likewise, if I was happy, I would sing to Him. If I was content, I would sing to Him. When I was at ease, I would sing to Him. I fell asleep almost every night singing to Jesus. When I sang to Him, I felt loved and at peace.

Looking back on those precious nights, I see now what I may not have fully realized at the time: a divine exchange was occurring during those moments. I was laying my feelings at the foot of the cross. I was pouring my heart out to my Savior through song, and in exchange, He was giving me peace. He was pouring His love and strength into me. He was my safe place. He was staking a claim on my heart as my first love.

In essence, I was experiencing the gospel in action. I was walking out my relationship with Him, a loving relationship where I trusted Him with my burdens, and then His grace strengthened me to live for Him. It is through Jesus that I also began to love and trust my Abba Father, became filled with the Holy Spirit, and began to learn and walk in His ways.

The more time I spent in God's presence, the more my heart healed, too. His love fills those places in our hearts where the mistakes of others and the cares of this world had once ripped open gaping holes. Those old themes of feeling neglected, rejected, and overlooked fell off me. He never leaves and is always there. He always understands. There is never a time when He doesn't see me.

In my midtwenties, during an extended hospital stay because of paralysis, guess what I was doing every night? Yes, singing to my Savior. In my spirit, I was still running into His lap for a hug.

I still spend as much time connecting with Jesus as possible, whether it is through singing, journaling, or speaking to Him throughout the day.

Some days, my heart is overflowing with joy. Life feels full. It's as if an entire symphony orchestra is playing the soundtrack of my life with ease. It's beautiful. It's real. And I can't wait to enter the presence of Jesus to share it with Him. In those moments, I literally feel like flying on eagles' wings!

On difficult days, my heart feels like it's being choked by the disappointments of life and the chaos of the world. It may take all of my strength to calm my mind enough to make an audible sound. And once I do, it's just my little voice, crying out as I sing once again to the familiar tune of "Jesus Loves Me."

It may not feel like it, but those moments are also beautiful and real. Jesus is waiting for me with open arms every single time.

There was even a season when I thought the song in my heart had ended. Sorrow crept into places where life once lived and, if kept unchecked for too long, will attempt to silence you. This happened to me, and it caused such grief. As I look back, I wonder if things could have been different. Maybe if I had kept singing through it all... Maybe if I had refused to become silent... Maybe if I had been stronger... Maybe...

As I brought my regret to Jesus, He gently reminded me He never left my side. He missed my voice during those dark days, but He never forgot my song. He had been singing over me even when I found myself too weak to join in.

"The Lord your God in your midst, The Mighty One, will save; He will rejoice over you with gladness, He will quiet you with His love, He will rejoice over you with singing."
~ Zephaniah 3:17, NKJV

My name may have once been "Mourning Song" but now He knows me as "Morning Song."

The time of grief and regret was over and we could now rejoice together!

Over the years, I've learned time with God isn't meant to be only a moment-to-moment experience, but a lifelong experience. We don't have to wait until a specific time of day to speak with Him. This shared dialogue can be ongoing. The divine exchange is always available to us at all times.

> "But I will sing of Your power; Yes, I will sing aloud of Your mercy in the morning; For You have been my defense And refuge in the day of my trouble."
> ~ Psalm 59:16, NKJV

Jesus has always been the one to open the right doors for me. He has always been the one to encourage, guide, and direct me. He always welcomes me home with open arms. It is He who ushers me into the very presence of God. Even now, words escape me as I can't adequately describe Him. My human attempts pale in comparison with all that Jesus is and all that He does! I could go on and on about Jesus, and it will truly never be enough.

Whatever you are going through, however you may feel, don't hold back from Jesus. We can ask Him to give us faith like a child. He desires to be our first love. The ugly or painful things you've kept hidden will lose their power as you present them to Him, for He is bigger than anything you may be facing. Share your heart with Him. Push through any hesitation.

Step into the melody of His presence. Feel the rhythm of His heartbeat. You can trust Him. He is fully capable and completely worthy to be praised!

> "Come to Me, all you who labor and are heavy laden, and I will give you rest. Take My yoke upon you and learn from Me, for I am gentle and lowly in heart, and you will find rest for your souls. For My yoke is easy and My burden is light."
> ~ Matthew 11:28-30, NKJV

LET'S TALK ABOUT FAITH

1. How does your faith impact the burdens you carry?

2. What is your earliest memory of Jesus?

3. Does music influence your walk with Christ?

4. Could you relate to Karen's testimony?

THE GOSPEL FOR TODAY

No matter what life throws our way, we are never in it alone. Jesus is "Immanuel,"[2] God with us.

---

[2] Matthew 1:23

CHAPTER 17
CHOOSING GOD

Dr. Wemi Omotosho

"What's wrong with your eye?" she asked, the puzzlement evident on her face. Then, almost immediately, she seemed to catch herself. "Oh yeah, I remember you said you were ill."

I nodded and smiled brightly beneath my face mask, but then I remembered that the "squint" was only evident whenever I smiled—or chewed, or yawned, or many other facial expressions that I had taken for granted for so long. I hurried through the pleasantries and took my leave.

Just a few minutes before Sunday service began, I finished going through the worship team sound check on stage and spied my friend in the auditorium. Between her moving away and the multiple lockdowns of the previous year, I hadn't seen her in approximately two years. However, in just a few seconds, the excitement I had felt at seeing her again dimmed as I wished it wasn't still obvious there was something not quite right with my face.

I had fallen ill with Bell's Palsy in December 2019 and lost the use of one side of my face. The unilateral facial paralysis was supposedly temporary. However, thirteen months later, I still had the same burning questions: When will my face fully recover? What if it gets to a certain point and my healing comes to a halt?

As I headed back to the stage that morning, I wondered, and not for the first time, why I was putting myself through this. As an introvert, I hated anything that made me the center of attention. And that was without the palsy. But I knew God still wanted me to use my voice for Him, so I did my best to ignore the roar and clamor of my fears and worries and continued to attend weekly rehearsals and sing on stage on Sundays with the rest of the worship team, squint, stiff facial muscles, and all.

It would be much easier to just wait until I was fully recovered, however long that took, if ever. But whenever I'm tempted to stay hidden in the shadows to avoid uncomfortable stares and awkward questions, my heart echoes these words from the psalmist:

> "Whom have I in heaven but you?...My flesh and my heart may fail, but God is the strength of my heart and my portion forever."
> ~ Psalm 73:25-26, NIV

Over the preceding twelve months, as I learned to straddle the line between lament and joy, my faith in God kept me tethered and grounded when storms threatened to blow me away. Reading His Word daily has shaped my attitude and perspective to help me live my life in a meaningful, authentic, and courageous way.

Looking back on what has arguably been one of the most challenging seasons in my life, I can see, contrary to my initial feelings of hopelessness, God's hand has been at work. He has been faithful. I have made immense progress in my recovery, and He has used those same circumstances to deepen my faith and knowledge of Him.

I wish I could say that I sailed through every challenge and rocky terrain with grace and without murmurings, but I didn't (and still don't). There have been many days of tears, fears, and wavering hope. However, on those days, I can "cast all my anxiety on Him because He cares for me."[1] Having faith in God means I can invite Him into the most painful realities of my life, just as I am. He doesn't need me to keep it together and put on a bold face. Serving a God who tends to His children lovingly, even to the point of giving up His only Son, means I can let down my guard before Him to find refreshment and reprieve.

My faith keeps me holding on to Him even when things don't seem to go my way or when it seems my prayers are not being answered. I am comforted when I remember these words from Romans 8:28, "And we know [with great confidence] that God [who is deeply concerned about us] causes all things to work together [as a plan] for good for those who love God, to those who are called according to His plan and purpose."[2] Even as life's events leave me bewildered, I hold on to this truth.

My belief in the only one God and the work of Christ Jesus on the cross involves a daily moment-by-moment surrendering of my will through the help of the Holy Spirit to do God's will. Despite the challenges that may come each day, my faith is underpinned by His promise in Hebrews 13:5, that "I will never [under any circumstances] desert you [nor give you up nor leave you without support, nor will I in any degree leave you helpless], nor will I forsake or let you down or relax My hold on you [assuredly not]!"[3] Because of this, I try to live each day in a way that persists and

---

[1] 1 Peter 5:7, NIV
[2] AMP
[3] Hebrews 13:5b, AMP

permeates like Jesus and is ultimately dependent and obedient to God.

LET'S TALK ABOUT FAITH

1. How can you cling to Jesus when life doesn't go as planned?

2. Could you relate to Wemi's testimony?

THE GOSPEL FOR TODAY

No matter how chaotic or shaky our lives get, God is never failing and unchanging.

CHAPTER 18

THE LOVE OF THE WORD

Jessica Schneider

Do you love the Bible? Please answer honestly. If you are having a Bible study or book club with this book, please share your answer with those in your group, and why.

Here is my honest answer: I didn't, but now I do.

I used to feel envious of people who *loved* their Bible and couldn't get through the day unless they were in the Word. I didn't understand them, so I was good just serving Him. I didn't see the need to be in His Word at all.

Besides, I already knew what the Bible said. And let's be honest, it's hard to read verses like "in this world you will have trouble,"[1] because we want life to be sunshine and rainbows. I didn't want to read scriptures telling me to be strong and courageous,[2] to forgive those who wronged me,[3] or to be still and trust that He is God.[4] I definitely didn't want to read scriptures that encouraged me to have faith when I

---

[1] John 16:33
[2] Joshua 1:9
[3] Ephesians 4:32
[4] Psalm 46:10

couldn't see the next step. I didn't want to step out of the boat when the waves could drown me[5] or endure for the sake of the cross!

Be nice to your enemies.[6] Let God fight the battles that, to the human eye, He doesn't seem to be fighting.[7] Be obedient even when it doesn't seem like the best way.[8] I didn't want to read any of that.

But my mindset changed during a small group Bible study about four years ago. We were supposed to begin the study by reading text from the Book of John, but two young women in the group didn't know how to find the Gospels, or any other book, for that matter. If that is you, please know it's okay!

So, we scrapped the study to show the ladies how to find the different books of the Bible, and where to begin if they had never read it before (the psalms or a Gospel is my suggestion). I noticed that one of the women owned a really old version of the Bible that was hard to understand, so that night I ordered her a version that was easier to read.

She brought it with her to study the next week, hugged it to her chest, and said, "this belongs to me." She knew it was a precious gift, not from me, but from a good Father. She knew the book was written for her. That changed my perspective on the Bible. I thought, "Yeah, this is for me," and I prayed for a love of His Word.

Soon after, one of my best friends started a journey neither of us expected. She said, "I am accountable to you," and started sending me her Bible study notes every day. As I got into His Word more often, I sent her my notes. To this day, we still study the Word of God together and send each other our notes and personal reflections on Scripture. But this still isn't when I began to love His Word.

---

[5] Matthew 14:24-33
[6] Romans 12:14
[7] Romans 12:19
[8] Isaiah 55:9

I knew the importance of being in Scripture. I loved studying the Bible because I got to know more about who our unfailing Father is. I loved learning things I had never noticed before, even in the stories I knew since I was a child.

But I still didn't truly love my Bible or take delight in God's Word.

That all changed early in 2021 when my friend left me the perfect gift. She always gave me thoughtful gifts, but this gift left me speechless. She left it for me when I came to take her dogs out one night: a perfectly wrapped, beautiful, large, white Bible.

Now, I have like ten Bibles, but none of them hold any particularly special meaning to me because I bought them myself. But I have always wanted one that held more sentiment, something more meaningful.

I never told my friend or anyone else about my wish. I never even prayed about it, but God knew the desires of my heart. He knew I would treasure the gift and hold it carefully. He knew I would let tears fall at the beauty of the gift and thankfulness for the friend who gave it to me. I immediately loved the Bible, and I loved what was written in it.

Later that same day, I came across Psalm 119, where the psalmist wrote about delighting in God and His Word. This is when I began to look forward to my time in my Bible every day, to truly love His Word. I finally understood what it meant to delight in God's Word!

I now know it in my heart: God's Word can be something to enjoy. His Word is good, trustworthy, tested, and it stands firm in heaven. His Word is to be kept, guarded, and observed.

We can not only study His Word, but we can also delight in it, because it was written for us so to know who our loving Father is. His Word is to be treasured. It helps us see His commands are good and wonderful. His Word strengthens our weary souls. We can find comfort in His Word, and in salvation. The Bible is a light for our path, our delight despite circumstances. His Words are sweeter than honey. Most importantly, His Word is all about Jesus and the hope we can have because of His sacrifice.

We can take delight in studying God's Word simply because it belongs to you.

LET'S TALK ABOUT FAITH

1. Do you have a Bible that's special to you?

2. How does your faith impact the way you read the Bible?

3. Could you relate to Jessica's testimony?

THE GOSPEL FOR TODAY

The Bible is the living Word of God. It is alive and active[9] and Jesus can use it to speak to our hearts.

---

[9] Hebrews 4:12

CHAPTER 19

MOM LIFE

Heather Hart

Being a parent is hard, and each family has their own dynamics. But here's the thing: Regardless of what your family looks like, we all have the same Jesus, and He can help us through anything.

Personally, I have five teenagers. Life is never dull at the Hart house, that's for sure. From football practice and frenemies to new drivers and braces, we run the gauntlet. And there are usually video games, YouTube videos, or music involved. But there's also a whole lot of Jesus.

> "Train up a child in the way he should go; even when he is old he will not depart from it."
> ~ Proverbs 22:6, ESV

He shows up in the form of grace when my kids fail, fall short, or have a bad day.

He's there during guitar lessons, church services, and Bible studies.

Jesus is there during every crisis, at every doctor visit, and every moment in between.

Jesus is there when our kids interact with their friends at school or online. Because Jesus is our foundation at home, He is the foundation their lives are built upon. Even if they haven't made that decision yet.

And that's something else. That decision they haven't all made, years ago I realized their salvation isn't up to me. God can save them despite my best efforts, or because of them. The choice is His, and His alone.

Here are two other moms who wanted to take a moment to share their hearts.

Making Peace with Time

Dr. Karen Michelle Ricci

Time. You can waste it, lose it, manage it, and even try to save it. But the one thing you can't do is cheat it, no matter how much you may want to.

It's funny how the passage of time changes as we get older.

The hot summer days of Texas lasted so long during my childhood. They seemed to drag on forever. They were as long as the temperatures were hot. Swimming. Sunburns. Running barefoot through the grass (until I got a splinter in my foot—an often occurrence). Time was ample, and I didn't understand its value. I carelessly used it in excessive quantities, even deep into my twenties.

Most of those days are just a blur now, just a blip in my life. Sure, some memories stand out more than others. But they are far from me. The sights, smells, and feelings of days gone by bleed together like watercolors on paper, forming what we refer to as our "past."

There are some days when time stood still, days with huge, ginormous moments that will never be forgotten. We've all encountered the type of moments that were so significant that somehow their very existence supersedes time, and now they sit in our minds like some immovable thing, solidly fixed. They are like tent stakes pounded down into the corner of our minds, firmly holding a memory in place for years to come, perhaps even for an entire lifetime.

The day I found out I was pregnant was one of those days. Less than a year earlier, I lay paralyzed in a hospital bed. The future was uncertain and I was told, due to a specific type of medical treatment, that I'd be rendered completely infertile. The doctor said it and I believed it.

But there I was, sitting in the bathroom, staring at a pregnancy test, clearly reading a positive result. A joy unspeakable welled up inside me and poured out as tears. Happy tears are different from sad ones… less heavy on the face and easier to see through.

Nine months later entered our Isabella. Little girls are wonderful. They flit about with wings, singing and moving in and out of imaginary worlds of their own creation. Then they share these worlds with those who love them, unabashedly, without reservation. That was our little girl. She was the miracle child we didn't try for because we hadn't thought it even possible. Sometimes God meets desires we aren't aware of or even working toward. And He does it because He loves us.

Until she was the age of four, the days seemed long. The feeding, cleaning, changing… you know the deal. It's all wonderful but can be tiring. Once out of the toddler years, however, it all began to slip by so quickly.

Diapers changed to big girl pants. Velcro changed to shoelaces. Learning the alphabet changed to short stories, reading novels, writing words, and then writing her own stories.

Adulthood is almost staring us in the face now. It's just around the corner. It's coming and coming rapidly in my daughter's life. Oh, how I wish we could slow time. That's the heart of a mom talking. It may be a bit of fear talking, too. I won't lie. Sometimes I wonder if my husband and I have done enough. Have we taught her all we could? Will she be ready to be an adult? Will she stay close to God? What will the world be like then? Will she be okay, more than okay?

It is in these moments that I run to my Abba Father. Even at my age, He fathers me. He draws me in close to His heart and reminds me His hand has been on my child since before she was conceived. Before she was my child, she was His child. He has a plan for her life, and I can trust Him with that.

"For I know the thoughts that I think toward you, says the Lord, thoughts of peace and not of evil, to give you a *future and a hope*."
~ Jeremiah 29:11, NKJV
(emphasis added)

Yes, time is going by much quicker than I'd like. Making the most of these days is one of my main goals as a parent, especially now. But time isn't an enemy I must cheat or grieve the passing of. It is merely a tool that aids me in creating as many good memories and learning moments as possible. It is the vehicle that opens up the space needed to point my daughter to Jesus, walk in God's ways, and know without a shadow of a doubt that she is eternally loved and treasured by Him.

We may not know exactly what the future holds for us or our children. But we can rest in Him, knowing that He is the Lord of time. All of our days are in His hands. He knows the beginning from the end. He is actively involved in our lives, healing us from our yesterdays, walking us through our todays, and patiently waiting for us in our tomorrows.

TRUSTING JESUS

Laura J. Marshall

Sitting outside on the steps of the deck, the sun warmed my tired, bare feet.

I'm staying with my oldest son for a few more days, then it's on to the next guest room.

A short-time homeless situation.

Four more weeks, give-or-take, and then I'd have somewhere to call home again.

No one can prepare you to suddenly leave your home in search of a borrowed place to lie your head.

Looking up, I see the large trees beyond my son's home moving in the strong wind that blows through.

It sounds like highway rush hour. Yet on the top of a mountain on ten acres, it's more like the breath of God.

I worry about my sons and about staying with family. I worry about things I cannot control.

Like the large tree swaying and bending toward my son-and daughter-in-law's bedroom.

Shall I worry for ten years, every night until it falls?

Twisting my hands, fretting, losing sleep, and shortening my life?

There are so many things we cannot control in the world.

The way of the wind.

The influences of the world on … everything or everyone we love.

The last thing I should be writing while separated from my children is something on parenting.

But I will tell you …

Seeds grow.

And your influence and values.

Live on in the lives you planted them into.

And the care of your sons and daughters couldn't be in more capable hands than those of a loving God.

LET'S TALK ABOUT FAITH

1. How does your faith impact your parenting?

2. Did you relate more to Karen or Laura's testimony?

THE GOSPEL FOR TODAY

God holds our children in His hands. He loves them even more than we do and can work in their lives despite our best efforts, failures, and doubts.

CHAPTER 20

FAITH THROUGH THE STORM

Jessica Schneider

I would never be the one to say that I hope God leads me through a category five hurricane. But going through a category five hurricane changed my life. It taught me to walk by faith alone, to tell God I wanted to walk through life like we walked through Hurricane Maria. Oh, my dear friends, that was a dangerous statement taken seriously by God.

That was in the fall of 2017. In truth, I said it with full confidence in Him. I learned that He is surely in even the tiniest of details of His plan, even though the road may be painful.

But let me start from the beginning.

My husband and I went to Puerto Rico to stay at my aunt and uncle's house to celebrate our five-year wedding anniversary. We honeymooned in Puerto Rico, and I'd visited my aunt and uncle's house there at least eight times over the years. It felt like home to me.

I had just finished reading a book about fear, and during my first morning at the beach, I decided I was done with it. So, I did something that I am pretty afraid of: I went diving through the waves. I'd shied away from waves with any amount of power for fifteen years because I got pounded by a wave when I lived in California.

I had just told God I was done with fear, no matter what came my way. And that is when news of a strengthening hurricane was headed straight for Puerto Rico. By the next morning it had grown into a category three, and then by that night it was a category five hurricane named Maria.

We tried to get off the island. We were willing to leave all our possessions, drive across the island to San Juan, and get a flight to anywhere on the East Coast. But that didn't happen. Every time the customer service woman found a flight for us, and clicked "Book," the seats disappeared.

God could have gotten us off the island, but He didn't. And He didn't because He knew that growing our faith through the storm was more important than getting us home before the storm.

The house was secure, but the storm was strong. I had never seen rain blow sideways or heard the wind howl like that. And I have never been so unafraid. I remember standing in front of the side door as the wind pounded the house, threatening to knock the door down, thinking, "I should be afraid, but I am not."

The storm seemed to last forever, and when it ended, the devastation was unimaginable. It was like we were on the set of Hollywood's latest disaster movie. All communication was down. There was no internet, TV, radio, phones, or electricity (except we had a great generator!). There was no way to let anyone in the outside world know we were okay, and no way of knowing when we would get home.

It took a while to figure out what to do. Then we heard the airport in San Juan was open, so our best bet was to drive across the devastated island (with no GPS), in hopes of finding a flight home. We immediately packed our bags, packed the rental car, and left, not knowing when we would get home, or what was ahead.

On the way to San Juan, we drove through deep waters of a flooded highway. In that moment, I realized I was experiencing the truth of God's promise in Isaiah 43:2.

> "When you go through deep waters, I will be with you. When you go through rivers of difficulty, you will not drown. When you walk through the fire of oppression, you will not be burned up; the flames will not consume you."
> ~ Isaiah 43:2, NLT

If I can summarize the verse in a few words, it would be this: He takes care of us and protects the faithful. Just as quickly as we packed up our stuff and left, God took care of us and provided for every detail when we got to San Juan.

We had a really nice hotel with full power (fully paid for), a good meal, and hot showers. Then we got confirmation of a flight home two days later, along with a way to tell our loved ones in the States we were okay.

I wish I could sit with you and tell you how God was in every single tiny detail of getting us home safely. They are countless, intricate, and perfectly planned. But I will leave it with this.

God was so faithful. And His faithfulness through it all led me to tell Him I wanted to walk through life like we walked through Hurricane Maria, not knowing what was ahead, but trusting He would take care of it all.

I also wish I could tell you everything that has happened over the past couple of years since Maria as I have stepped out of my boat called "safety," and into the wind and the waves. I wish I could tell you all the decisions I have made in faith that are foolish by human standards. I have been called stupid and naïve. I've heard comments like, "Well, things don't seem so great now, do they?" I've seen people around me just waiting for me to fail and say that I made a mistake in stepping out in faith.

And I have seen what happens when we step out in faith as He asks us to.

I have seen God move mountains. I have seen His name glorified. I have stood in a room filled with women, knowing without a doubt that I had trusted His Word. I was exactly where He wanted me, even though I'd been drowning in uncertainty only a few months earlier.

I have seen that He is faithful, and He does not make mistakes. My faith has been tested, and I have said that this faith thing feels too hard. But He has always been God, because He is the same yesterday, today, and tomorrow. It isn't a question, but a truth.

Faith isn't anything that you can put your hands on. As I write this, I don't know what is ahead. I feel like I am either in the storm again or nearing the end, waiting for Him to show the way, but not wanting to waste the waiting, either.

Nothing is certain right now. Hopefully, by the time you read this, things will be more clear. Until then, I just want Him to find me trusting in Him, abiding in Him, the one who goes before me, Jesus. The one who will again show that He will take care of every single little intricate detail, as I follow in faith.

I would never hope or pray that God would lead you to walk through a category five hurricane. But my prayer for you is that He finds you abandonedly trusting in Him, and walking by faith alone, even through the strongest storm.

LET'S TALK ABOUT FAITH

1. Does your faith surface when you get scared?

2. How do we "waste the waiting?"

3. Could you relate to Jessica's testimony?

THE GOSPEL FOR TODAY

God protects those who belong to Him. Life might be hard, but we can trust in Jesus no matter how bad it gets.

Chapter 21

A Friend Who is Always by My Side

Sharon Hazel

I was driving home from work after another day in the office, looking forward to a relaxing evening with the family. Winter was drawing in. There had been sunshine earlier, but as the sun set, and it was getting cold and dark.

When I arrived at the house, I found our two teenage boys were on their own. My husband left a note to say he had gone for a walk, which was not unusual. As I organized dinner, I noticed it started to rain. I became concerned about my husband because he left without his coat. I tried ringing his mobile phone, but there was no reply.

Time seemed to pass quickly, and it was now dark, cold, and raining with a strong wind. I could not settle and felt prompted to look for him. I told the boys I was going out for a quick drive to see if I could find their father and give him a lift home. As I got ready, I said a quick prayer, "Lord, help me find him," and then I set out.

Prayer is simply talking with Jesus. It is not one way, if we listen, we will see and hear Him speak to us in a very personal way. He is not remote or distant. It is amazing but true that He is interested in the day-to-day details of our lives, and more than that, He is there with us! One of my favorite Bible verses is Psalm 46:1, "God is our refuge and strength, an ever-present help in trouble," because it has been a comfort and a truth in my life.

I decided to drive my husband's usual walking route, a six-mile circuit along the coast. He usually turned left at the end of our road, but as I arrived at the intersection, the thought dropped into my mind to go the other way, to turn right. I hesitated at the intersection. There were no other cars around, and my logic told me to go left. That is the walk he liked, the way he always went. But I felt God whispering to me, not audibly, but a still persistent inner voice, to turn right.

I listened, and with another quick prayer, I turned right onto a winding single track. It was an unlit country lane, and it was there, a few miles along, that I found my husband unconscious on the road. He had slipped and fallen, and he had a cut on the front and on the back of his head. I later learned he had a few broken ribs and a severe concussion.

I could not move him, so I called for an ambulance. They immediately assessed that he had hypothermia, as well as his other injuries. They took him to the hospital, where he was admitted overnight. He was released the next day, bandaged and bruised, with strict instructions to rest quietly at home.

My faith is not about religion; it's all about relationship. I believe I have a friend in Jesus who is always with me. On that night, He prompted me to go out looking for my husband, and He directed me to the right place, at the right time, just when help was needed.

What do you expect from a friendship? Usually, a friend is someone with similar interests, who we find it easy to talk to, and who will listen to what we have to say. A good friendship develops over time as we share good and bad experiences together. A true friend will speak the truth, someone who will tell us not what we want to hear, but what we need to know. We trust our friends to watch out for us, and to defend and protect us. These are high expectations of friendship, and we will rarely live up to such an ideal, but there is one true friend who will never let us down.

Jesus calls us friends. We become His friends when we acknowledge Him as our Lord and Savior. We can start a relationship with a true and trusted friend, one like no other, who we can rely on and depend on, through all the ups and downs of life, a friend who will always be by our side. A friend we can talk to, who is always available to listen. A friend who speaks into our lives today, mainly through His Word in the Bible, but sometimes through other people and their stories, or even through our own thoughts. When Jesus speaks to us, it will always be through love, as revealed and confirmed in His Word:

> "My command is this: Love each other as I have loved you. Greater love has no one than this: to lay down one's life for one's friends. You are my friends if you do what I command."
> ~ John 15:12-14, NIV

Jesus' commands are not difficult, just simply to love God and to love one another.

> "And surely I am with you always, to the very end of the age."
> ~ Matthew 28:20, NIV

LET'S TALK ABOUT FAITH

1. Have you thought about your faith being more like a relationship than a religion?

2. Could you relate to Sharon's testimony?

THE GOSPEL FOR TODAY

God isn't some supernatural being looking down on us from above. He is real and wants to have a personal relationship. And that relationship is on solid ground. He will never unfriend us.

CHAPTER 22
FAITH & CHURCH

Mariel Davenport

Bewildered, I sat on the hard pew, lost in my own thoughts. "Why do we have to go to church on Easter? Why are these people following these silly rituals?" Stand, sit, kneel, only to stand again. The aerobics classes I've seen my mom participate in seemed more entertaining than this. As a teenager, I found no value in the counterfeit traditions the church seemed to offer.

I grew up in a home where escaping to my room was a necessary but lonely reprieve, even for my introverted self. The alternative, being in the same room as the stepfather I loathed, was unthinkable. So alone I sat, escaping into books and phone conversations with the few friends I let into my life. My introverted mindset led me down many roads of contemplative thought. Or maybe it was the brokenness within that compelled me to solve my own issues.

Either way, I determined early on that church and the rituals it carried were unnecessary for me. The requirements of dressing up, acting a certain way, and enduring dagger looks from my mother when my brother and I giggled too loudly weren't worth whatever it was this place had to offer.

From my vantage point, they talked too much, sang words that didn't seem to matter, and passed a plate asking for money like a street beggar. None of it made sense, but at least it was a rarity for us.

SHIFTING

My small-town man and I married in our early twenties. He insisted on bowing his head to pray before meals, despite my scoffing. And when the faint line on the pregnancy test appeared just a few months into marriage, his desire for church grew. Having been raised in the rhythm of weekly church attendance, dutifully sitting next to his grandfather with open Bibles and organ music floating through the air, he held the routine near to his heart. As my belly grew, so did his insistence for us to find a church.

We navigated the crowd awkwardly from the parking lot to the pew. My man had suggested the church down the road because the denomination was the one he grew up in. I didn't argue—much. Clinging to his hand, I waddled through the musty smelling hallways toward the sanctuary. Something about this place felt comforting, not like the random churches of my youth.

Though I don't remember the pastor's sermon, I do remember the shift within me one Sunday morning as I sat next to my husband, belly filling my lap. The pastor offered free Bibles to anyone interested. Something in me was compelled by the offer. As we left the sanctuary that Sunday, we paused at the table of Bibles, and the nice lady handed me a paperback Bible with a smile. It would be months before I opened its pages. But I felt drawn back to the sanctuary each week.

The baby came, our routines were overturned, and the church visits paused. One morning a neighbor we had spoken to at church knocked on the door. When I opened it,

I was greeted with a basket of goodies. The note said, "Congratulations on the new baby! Here is my number if you ever have a need, but please do not write me a thank you note for this." It was signed in her handwriting. I felt hugged in a way I had not experienced before. Unpacking the treasures, I found homemade bread carefully wrapped in foil and ribbon, along with a new mom devotional, a candle, a gift card and an invitation to their book group, along with a copy of the book.

I couldn't get back to church fast enough the next Sunday. I felt graced, loved, seen.

SURRENDERING

I surrendered my life to Christ the following month. When His light broke through my atheist heart, my husband's routine religion cracked and he, too, surrendered to a true relationship with Jesus. We were baptized together that following year while our eighteen-month-old was cared for by the older lady in the nursery.

The churches of our early married life offered nothing different from the churches of my youth, and yet everything was different. I'd found a home at church. Witnessing the body of Christ in action shifted something in me that drove me straight to the feet of my Savior. I found much more than a building that smelled like an old library. I found a family that encouraged my faith and pursuit of Jesus.

In the decades since, the culture of our family has included the bi-weekly drive to church, and many years growing, failing, encouraging, laughing, crying, serving and living within its walls and with His people. I felt a redeemed harvesting of fruit from a branch that had been long since dried up the day each of my boys surrendered their own lives to Christ. Church has been the greenhouse where my tender faith, and the faith of my man and sons, has been nurtured and trained to bear fruit. The people there aren't perfect. Never have been. The experiences have held hurts, disappointments, and failed expectations. But the gathering of believers, the united songs of worship to our God, and the sharpening of souls has been life-giving in ways that far outweigh the afflictions.

Faith has been the lens through which this once-atheist found life within the walls of a church building.

LET'S TALK ABOUT FAITH

1. How does your faith impact your church attendance?

2. Why do you go to church?

3. Could you relate to Mariel's testimony?

THE GOSPEL FOR TODAY

Even when we are running, we have a God that pursues us.[1]

---

[1] Genesis 3:9

Chapter 23
Marriage & Faith

Jaime Hampton

In our twenty-two years of marriage, my husband and I have gone through ups, downs and all-arounds. We've lived in four different states and seven different homes. We've been through earthquakes, births, deaths, job loss, tragedy, laughter, and tears. We're about as different from one another as two people could be, and we've had more disagreements than we can remember.

It's been a crazy journey, but the one constant in all of it has been faith.

At times, we have very different outlooks on God and life, but we have both placed our faith in Jesus. So, when I was asked the question of how faith impacts marriage, my first thought is that it's the glue that holds our marriage together. It's the rock we stand on when we're surrounded by quicksand. The truth we cling to when voices around us are telling us our needs aren't being met, we deserve more, or there is romance and happily ever-after somewhere other than with each other. Faith is the driving force pulling us toward each other when the enemy is grabbing from all sides trying to rip us apart.

While all of these metaphors have been true for me and my husband, it would be foolish for me to package all that up and tie it with a bow. Women with tremendous faith are living in failing marriages, especially if that faith is one-sided. If you're struggling through an unwanted separation or divorce, please know my heartfelt prayers are with you. But even in these heart-wrenching situations, even through the valley of the shadow of death of a marriage, faith can keep you standing in prayer. Even if those prayers are raging, angry prayers to a God you feel is cruel for not using His infinite power to mend the brokenness. Even when there are no words to speak, faith summons the Spirit who intercedes "with groans too deep for words,"[1] carrying the deepest needs, dreams, and desires of your heart to a God who sees, hears, and works.

When I think about what my marriage would be like if I didn't have the teachings of Jesus and the Holy Spirit living in me, I realize I would be far more self-centered. Not to say that I'm not still selfish or me-centered in my marriage at times; I'm so far

> "And we know that in all things God works for the good of those who love him, who have been called according to his purpose."
> ~ Romans 8:28, NIV

from perfect it's not funny. But because of my faith, rather than viewing marriage as a union designed to fill me, "complete me," and bring me joy and contentment, I see it as a covenant through which God blesses me, sharpens me, betters me, and makes me more like Jesus.

Sometimes it's amazing, fun, and fulfilling. And sometimes it hurts. The amazing, fun, and fulfilling parts would be the same regardless of my faith. I've come to

---

[1] ISV

realize my faith defines what I do with the painful, uncomfortable, and inconvenient parts of marriage.

When I asked God how I could be a better wife, He gave me three ways to bless my husband. These three things have transformed me from the inside out, especially during the painful times when my wounded, deceitful heart[2] told me to disengage or avenge. And conveniently, these three things form an easy-to-remember acronym: YES.

Y: YIELD

The "Y" stands for yield. To yield is to surrender, submit, or give way.

It's important to yield to our husbands, and even more important to yield to the Holy Spirit who helps us yield to our husbands.

The word "yield," reminds me of a two-way traffic stop. Yielding is more than an obligatory pause before bulldozing forward. It means the other car has the right to make the first move. So, I need to wait, give the car plenty of room, and time to move forward. I need to *assume* the car is going to move, and even if the driver is distracted by the radio or his phone, I must wait until I see the driver look up. I may have to honk the horn to get his attention, but I need to know the driver is aware he has the right of way. The driver may wave me on, letting me go first, in which case I have no problem with moving forward, but that's his call.

Whether it's your husband or the Holy Spirit, yielding requires humility and self-control. It doesn't come easily for me, but allowing space for my husband to grow and lead has done infinitely more than nagging or taking control ever did.

---

[2] Jeremiah 17:9

E: ELEVATE

The "E" stands for elevate. The antonyms for elevate speak volumes about what elevating our husbands means: disgrace, disdain, put down.

At first glance, I felt like I did a good job of not disgracing, disdaining, or putting down my husband. But as I prayed over this word, I felt God asking, "what about in your thoughts and attitudes?"

Oh, those.

While I don't verbally put my husband down, I confess to habits of eye-rolling, muttering when I think nobody's listening, and thinking negative thoughts about him, particularly when we disagree. Learning to be intentional about elevating my husband in my thoughts, words, and actions has not only helped me see my attitude toward him transform, but he's a happier man because of it. The hard part is knowing that the converse is true, and although I have the best of intentions, I too often fall back into destructive habits and patterns. I'm so glad for God's grace, and for the strength and hope He gives me to get back up when I fail.

> "For though the righteous fall seven times, they rise again, but the wicked stumble when calamity strikes"
> ~ Proverbs 24:16, NIV

S: SUPPLICATE

The "S" stands for supplicate. This comes down to good, old-fashioned prayer. God convicted me in this area by asking, "Do you pray for your husband as much as you think negatively about him?"

In the 2014 movie *War Room* with Priscilla Shirer, Miss Clara addressed this poignantly and hilariously, pointing out that we can't expect to see God moving in our marriage if all we do is complain about our husband. One of my favorite quotes from Miss Clara is, "Very few of us know how to fight the right way."[3]

Satan would love nothing more than to distract us from prayer with complaining, and to convince us that our husband is the real enemy. So, we need to fight on our knees *for* our husbands and *for* our marriages—not *with* our husbands *about* our marriages!

So how does faith impact marriage? Ultimately, it removes the veil of deception from our worldly eyes, allowing us to see truth clearly. Faith shows us who our real enemy is. It helps us understand what we should—and shouldn't—expect in marriage. It shifts our focus from what we can get to what we can give.

Faith helps us fix our eyes on Jesus.

> "Therefore, since we are surrounded by such a great cloud of witnesses, let us throw off everything that hinders and the sin that so easily entangles. And let us run with perseverance the race marked out for us, fixing our eyes on Jesus, the pioneer and perfecter of faith. For the joy set before him he endured the cross, scorning its shame, and sat down at the right hand of the throne of God."
>
> ~ Hebrews 12:1-2, NIV

LET'S TALK ABOUT FAITH

1. How did Jaime challenge your view of marriage?

---

[3] *War Room.* Alex Kendrick. Kendrick Brothers, 2015. DVD.

2. How does your faith impact your marriage?

The Gospel for Today

God doesn't just care about our marriage; He is part of it and can help us overcome any challenge we face.

Chapter 24

Faith at Work

Sharon Gibson

"Are you a substitute teacher at the high school?" I spotted her brunette head peeking out of a VW. She had pulled alongside me as I walked to a store in a small strip mall.

"Yes, I am." I came up to her car window.

"I just wanted to let you know you had a big influence on me in high school. Because of your stories and encouragement, I decided to major in chemistry and be a teacher."

My heart filled with joy. "Thank you for telling me this. I felt a little down and needed to hear it."

She smiled. "I had a sense I should share this with you today."

I am a substitute teacher for my school district. One time I entered the high school classroom and a sophomore boy jumped up out of his seat, "Mrs. Gibson, can I write 'Be diligent' on the board?"

"Yes, you may!" I smiled as the realization came to me. I got through to some students!

From the time they are in fifth to sixth grade, I've taught students that if they are diligent in their studies, they will be successful. They will be successful not only in school, but in life. Even if they don't like a subject, they learn diligence as they discipline themselves to study.

The rewards of diligence and the encouragement to be diligent are clear in the Bible. This counters some of the negativity about school and encourages them to have a positive attitude about school.

My missionary parents raised me overseas and I've adopted seven teens from poverty backgrounds, most of them from Latin America. I've seen the consequences of a lack of education firsthand, so I share this perspective with my students. I tell them they need to realize how fortunate they are, take their studies seriously, and be grateful.

At the beginning of class, before I go over the teacher's assignments, I give them brief talks and use stories to engage them with the principles I teach. I make the expectations clear so I get better cooperation from them during class. From the beginning, I share my desire to treat them with respect and consideration and my expectation that they give the same to each other. I also want them to show respect and consideration for their valuable educational opportunities by staying quiet and focused. I've found this to be a good classroom management strategy. Once they are in high school, I share productivity tips that help them make the most of their education. I encourage them to use the ninety minutes they have to learn to focus.

I have to reinforce the guidelines I set, and discipline is difficult, but I set a tone of respect and care for them. When I discipline them, I let them know it is because I care for them and want what's best for them. This is consistent with Hebrews 12:6 about how God disciplines those He loves. Sometimes, I tell them that if they accept correction, they will be smart and will grow in knowledge and understanding.[1]

I've had students I've disciplined later wave at me in the hall or even give me a hug. Then I know I've been successful. Not all students respond like this. Some reject correction and end up in trouble. But those who accept correction settle down and improve their behavior. I've even had a couple of them write me apology notes or apologize in person.

Occasionally, I'm called to substitute during test day. Sometimes the teacher will write me a note of warning, "You have to watch them because they cheat." So, I usually give them a brief talk at the beginning about how the only ones they are cheating are themselves, because they don't know what they don't know on a test, but they will need to know the material for later tests. Then I tell them, "Whoever walks in integrity walks securely." I continue, "You will feel better about yourself and be more secure when you are honest."[2] After I share this truth, I am amazed at how little cheating I see.

One of my favorite things to encourage students is to develop their gifts, talents, and abilities. I love to do creative lettering, so I often write my name on the whiteboard in creative lettering. If I forget, sometimes they'll ask, "Mrs. Gibson, would you write your name pretty on the board?"

I point this out as an example to encourage them to discover what they like to do, and to take time to learn it. I've read that we're losing the ability to be creative in our culture because we're preoccupied with electronic devices. I encourage them to take time away from their cell phones and video games to learn a skill or develop a hobby.

Recently, I've been taking one of my books on "How to Write Your Story: Writing Skills to Captivate Your Reader,"

---

[1] Proverbs 15:32, ESV
[2] Proverbs 10:9, NIV

to use as an example. I tell them, "When you take the time to develop your gifts, talents, and abilities, you can not only find satisfaction yourself, but you can also benefit others."

My goal as a substitute teacher is to train them in righteousness (right living) and teach them how to be successful. I cannot refer to the Bible specifically, but I can share common-sense biblical principles for successful living. The Bible says to "Preach the word; be prepared in season and out of season; correct, rebuke and encourage with great patience and careful instruction."[3] You can easily and intentionally do this without citing the passage.

I am also an intercessor. I pray for the students and teachers. I pray for them to know the truth and that God will send His ministering angels to bring them to salvation. I pray God will orchestrate events and situations for the students to find their God-given destinies. I often pray that God will bless my day and direct His love through and to me.

I pray for wisdom, and I seek wisdom. Especially in the beginning of my journey as a substitute teacher, I needed wisdom in classroom management, so I talked to a teacher friend of mine and did a lot of reading. I would pray after hard days and God was faithful to give me wisdom. Proverbs 3:17 says, "Her ways are pleasant ways, and her paths are peace." I have found this to be true about wisdom, and I enjoy sharing wisdom wherever I go.

I love the fact that I can go from classroom to classroom and influence a lot of students. Sometimes I can see anywhere from 300 to 400 different students a week. I've been in our school district for seven years, so that gives me time to have some of them over the years and to get feedback from them.

One time the students applauded me when I entered the classroom. A few other times, they applauded after my talk. One high school girl told me, "I appreciate the wisdom you

---

[3] 2 Timothy 4:2, NIV

share with us." Another said, "You talk about things that matter." Sometimes I get sweet notes from the students, especially in the younger grades.

One night I was in Walmart and the customer service representative said a cheerful, "Hi Mrs. Gibson" then another student came up and greeted me warmly. Then another student said, "Mrs. Gibson taught me to write pretty!" Then the customer service rep said, "We love Mrs. Gibson!"

Sometimes I go to the grocery store and students wave at me from a car or yell out, "Hi Mrs. Gibson." I don't always recognize them because I have so many students, but I always smile and wave. These kinds of responses make me realize that I'm making a difference and I enjoy the favor I have. Their responses give me the strength and the energy to keep going.

I have found these verses to be true:

"Let love and faithfulness never leave you; bind them around your neck, write them on the tablet of your heart. Then you will win favor and a good name in the sight of God and man."
~ Proverbs 3:3-4, NIV

"A good name is rather to be chosen than great riches, and loving favor rather than silver and gold."
~ Proverbs 22:1, KJV

"May the favor of the Lord our God rest on us; establish the work of our hands for us— yes, establish the work of our hands."
~ Psalm 90:17, NIV

In Romans 12, Paul says we're not to follow the pattern of this world. When God's Word transforms us, we test and approve what His will is. We implement His wisdom and see that it works. In this way, we prove that God's ways are good.

In my work, I confirm that God's ways of wisdom are good. My faith impacts my work in a positive, transforming way for myself and my students!

LET'S TALK ABOUT FAITH

1. How does your faith impact your work?

2. Could you relate to Sharon's testimony?

THE GOSPEL FOR TODAY

God is always with us. He can give us the words we need in any situation.[4]

---

[4] Psalm 32:8

CHAPTER 25

A LIFE WORTH LIVING

Leisa Williams

I am a wife, mother, and teacher. If you were to visit me, you would see a professional working woman in a lovely home. On the outside, it appears I have it all together. I try not to hide behind a mask, as I once did. Who you see now is mostly now who I am, although sometimes I still protect myself from rejection because I'm afraid for people to see the real me. Oh, when will I learn I do not need to seek the approval of others?

I am blessed in so many ways. I have a loving husband, three beautiful children, and a daughter-in-law whom I deeply love. I also absolutely love Jesus, my Savior and Lord, who I'm learning to trust more deeply with each passing year.

I didn't just arrive where I am today, and I try not to take my life for granted. I am a work in progress. I struggle with the stress of fighting the injustices that are a part of my life. I struggle with ungodly, controlling responses caused by pain from my earlier years. I struggle to let go and let God. When it's difficult to move forward, I seek God sincerely and press into Him. Through it all, my eyes are on the one who paid the price for my sin.

My journey of healing has led me into the arms of my heavenly Father over and over again. Today I can confidently say and know deep within my heart that my Abba Father doesn't just like me; He deeply loves me, as His precious daughter.

I grew up in a Christian family knowing about God, but not really knowing Him. I love music, so I as a girl, I had hopes of attending a music school near home to become a flutist. I thought I'd been accepted to the Conservatorium off music, so I was devastated when my name was not on the class list. My dreams were dashed, and I add struggled with deep depression over the uncertainty of my future. Then my mother's friend slipped a card with this Scripture into my hands as she was leaving our home one day.

> "But they who wait for the Lord shall renew their strength; they shall mount up with wings like eagles; they shall run and not be weary; they shall walk and not faint."
>
> ~ Isaiah 40:31

I clung to the hope those words gave me. Within a couple of weeks, I was offered a place at a music school far from home. After consultation with my parents, I nervously accepted the offer. Within a month, I left my hometown and my family to pursue my career in music.

At the tender age of seventeen, I was eight hours from home where everything was unfamiliar. I did not have the life skills to be thrust out into the world, but I had to learn quickly. I was very homesick, so the depression I'd struggled with at home came with me to college. And even though I loved learning music, I couldn't shake the overwhelming sadness inside me.

Early on, I met Cathy, who invited to take me to church on campus. I was lonely, so I accepted her offer. Church was not new to me, but the people at the university church were different. They took their relationship with God very seriously. He was not just part of their life; He was first and foremost in their lives. They read their Bible and really believed and lived out what was written in it. I was intrigued!

One weekend at church camp a guest speaker spoke on "First things first; second things second. Is Jesus Lord of your life?" The Holy Spirit convicted me that Jesus was not Lord of my life, that I was behind the wheel, not Him. That night I gave my life to Christ. I asked Him to move into the driver's seat, to forgive my sins, and to come into my heart so I could have a relationship with Him.

Cathy was so excited! She became a close friend and mentor as she answered so many questions. Throughout that time, I continued to struggle to connect to God. I felt like my prayers were hitting a brick wall and I experienced no breakthrough with emotional pain. Then one night as I was crying out to God I read Psalm 66:18: "If I had not confessed the sin in my heart, the Lord would not have listened."[1]

I realized I was still clinging to my old ways, not changing my life. I still watched rubbish on TV and drank too much wine, which affected my closeness with God. But it went deeper than my outward living. I harbored anger, hurt, pain, and bitterness over things that happened as a child. The inner emotions resulting from deep hurt and pain blocked an intimate relationship with my Heavenly Dad.

What a journey!

This baggage was not dealt with overnight. I have experienced so many twists and turns and bumps in the road, but God faithfully led me on His path of righteousness. Matthew 7:13-14 says, "Enter through the narrow gate. For wide is the gate and broad is the road that leads to

---

[1] NLT

destruction, and many enter through it. But small is the gate and narrow the road that leads to life, and only a few find it."[2]

If you and I had several hours to sit down over a cup of coffee, I would share what this deeper journey on a very narrow road looks like. I would share about the cost and the sacrifice, but most of all, about the intimacy I developed with Abba Father. After I shared how I came through my inner healing journey, I would share how my youngest son was diagnosed with autism and developmental delay. I would share how this kicked off a whole new journey between Abba and me.

I am now a middle-aged woman, and I still would never trade the love I have received that is like no other, for Jesus says, "I have said these things to you, that in me you may have peace. In the world you will have tribulation. But take heart; I have overcome the world"[3].

I have learned that He loves you, and He loves me, and this is only a snippet of my testimony.

LET'S TALK ABOUT FAITH

1. Do you realize you are a work in progress, or do you beat yourself up when you fail or fall short?

2. Do you have the peace Jesus offers in John 16:33?

3. How could you relate to Leisa's testimony?

---

[2] NIV
[3] John 16:33

THE GOSPEL FOR TODAY

When we confess our sins, they are washed away by the blood of Christ. We no longer have to live in shame or defeat. Through Christ we are forgiven and free.

CONCLUSION
THE GOSPEL FOR TODAY

Heather Hart

Have you ever wondered how to trust in Jesus when everything is falling apart? Sometimes we cling to Him when the going gets tough, and sometimes we wonder how things got so far out of control. Do you feel a longing to know Jesus more? To not simply know of Jesus, but to walk *with* Him?

Throughout the pages of this book, women have shared how the gospel, how Jesus, makes a difference in their lives every day. For the first time, or the ten thousandth time.

God is good and we can put our hope in the gospel each and every day. Here's what that looks like in real life:

- Even when I fall short or mess up, God's love and forgiveness never fails.
- No matter how out of control my life is, God is with me.
- No matter what life throws my way, I am never in it alone. Jesus is "Immanuel," God with us.
- No matter how chaotic or shaky my life gets, God is never failing and unchanging.

- The Bible is the living Word of God. It is alive and active, and Jesus can use it to speak to my heart.
- I want to live like Jesus, but even when I fail, I'm covered by the blood of Christ and there is no condemnation because I belong to Him.
- God holds my children in His hands. He loves them even more than I do and can work in their lives despite my best efforts, failures, and doubts.
- God protects those who belong to Him. Life might be hard, but I can trust in Jesus no matter how bad it gets.
- God isn't some supernatural being looking down on me from above. He is real and wants to have a personal relationship. And that relationship is on solid ground. He will never unfriend me.
- Even when I am running away from Jesus, I have a God that pursues me.
- God is always with me. He can give me the words I need in any situation.
- When I confess my sins, they are washed away by the blood of Christ. I no longer have to live in shame or defeat. Through Christ, I am forgiven and free.
- I didn't get enough done today, but at just the right time Jesus died for me, so I can trust that His timing is perfect.
- I really messed that up, but because of Christ, I am forgiven.
- I feel lonely and unloved, but I know Jesus loves me more than I can imagine (enough to live and die for me), and He is always with me.
- My son was born with cancer, but God can work all things together for His good. He watched His

Son die on the cross, and He can give me the strength to get through this (and He did).

- My husband left me for another woman, but the church is the bride of Christ, and He will never leave me.
- Life is hard, but Jesus conquered the grave and I have eternal life through Him.
- What I did was wrong, but Jesus came and died because He knew I was a sinner in need of a Savior.
- I failed to spend time with Jesus, but when I was a sinner, He still chose to die for me and though I forsake Him, He can never forsake Himself. Nothing I could ever do (or fail to do) can ever separate me from His love.

That's the power of the gospel. It can speak into any situation I face on any given day. It's what I can fall back on when my world is closing in. Jesus is unchanging. His love for me, and for you, seeped into the cross where He hung. It was sealed in the tomb where He laid. It is written in history and is bound in eternity.

That is the promise of the gospel. It saved me when I believed it, and it continues to save me every day. It gives me hope and reminds me who I am. It reminds me whose I am. It reminds me of my worth.

The gospel takes Jesus' perfection, His righteousness, and covers me with it. While I could never hope to be holy on my own, because of the gospel I am holy and precious in God's sight. That's a truth I can cling to no matter what life throws my way. And that's faith worth talking about.

WHO MOVED?

A Poem by Carlida Douthitt

There is a song that asks, "Who moved?
I am asking, have I moved?

Being in doubt/unbelief is a move away from God.
The way is dark, I'm all alone.
I'm out here, in the depths of despair
not a friend to care.

I thought I was doing what was right,
being loving, kind, taking care of everyone else,
trying to forget how much I wanted a friend
someone to listen to me and not judge me, to hold me tight
and say, "I will make everything right,"

I'd pray, talk to God, tell Him all my hurts and woes.
I knew He would listen, that He cared, and yet -
would He? Really?
I'd done things that seemed really unworthy.

I continue to make the same mistakes will I never learn?
How can He keep loving me when I can't love myself?

I built up walls between myself and God, between family and
friends.
I told myself that others only wanted to hurt me.
I worked hard to keep these walls in place,
never understanding that the more I kept them there,
the more no one could care.

I learned about treasures
only earthly treasures?
That where my treasure is,
that's also where my heart will be found.

Did I really want my heart to be in a garbage dump?
I learned how the mouth speaks,
how it only says what the heart tells it to say.
Does my mouth reflect my treasures,
of how unworthy, unlovable I am?

Yes, Lord, I moved.
I moved away from Your loving arms,
and away from Your Light.

Forgive me, Lord, for doubting You.
Forgive me for the walls I built,
teach me how to tear them down.
When I move back to You, You put Your arms around me.
You hold me tight and tell me You will make everything right.

Lord, You never move away from me;
any walls between us You never build.
You patiently wait for me to return,
and help me the walls to break.

Thank You, Lord, that Your word stays the same,
never changing, from beginning to end.
Teach me, Lord, to stay close by Your side,
and no more walls to build.

LIKE THIS BOOK?

Join the movement by sharing your struggles
and using them to point to Jesus—be sure to tag them
with #CandidlyChristian on social media.

Write a book review on Amazon,
your blog, and/or another online retailer.

Join our Facebook group
Facebook.com/Groups/CandidConversations

Visit our website, CandidlyChristian.com, where
women get candid about their life and faith every week.

Tell your friends and family about this book.

ABOUT THE AUTHOR

Heather Hart

Heather Hart is an award-winning author and member of the Association of Biblical Counselors. God has given her a heart for ministering to women of all ages; helping them grow in their walk with Christ. Her goal isn't to tell others how to do more, be better, or achieve perfection, it's to point them to Jesus.

Other Contributing Authors

Erika Bailey

Erika is the founder and president of The Round Farmhouse Ministries. She lives in a round farmhouse nestled in the hills of West Virginia with her husband, Travis, and their four children. Erika loves to dig into God's Word and make texts centuries old applicable today. Through her writings, she hopes to teach you more about God's Word, make you laugh, and possibly shed a tear or two (happy tears, of course). She prays that what she writes is relatable, encouraging, and brings you closer to the Lord as a result.

Theresa Boedeker

Theresa Boedeker is a storyteller, humor hunter, and encourager of others. She is passionate about helping women smash lies with God's truth and walk in freedom. She has two children and a husband. She enjoys taking pictures of flowers because they never try to get out of the picture. She unwraps life and faith at TheresaBoedeker.com where she reminds women what's important about life, themself, and grace.

Sarah J Callen

Sarah J Callen is an entrepreneur and published author, currently living in Dallas, Texas. Her dreams include founding businesses, giving strategically, and sharing art with the world. She believes that every number has a name, every name has a story, and every story is worthy of being shared.

Mariel Davenport

As an atheist transformed by the Word of God, Mariel Davenport knows the power of seeking God through His Word. Through her TEND method, a simple process of engaging with God through the Scriptures, Mariel seeks the Gardener and equips others to tend their soul by the Word. She shares her method through online TEND Gatherings, Scripture journals, and speaking engagements. Mariel is a wife of nearly 25 years, and a retired homeschool mama. You are invited to tend your soul with her bi-monthly newsletter, Tending Tools, and get updates and announcements about upcoming TEND Gatherings by signing up at marieldavenport.com/tending/

Carlida Douthitt

Carlida is a seventy-two-year-old woman who was raised in a Christian home. She wrote the poem "Who Moved?" around 1996, during a difficult time as a participant in a church group dealing with grief. She cared for her husband throughout a progressive illness until he died in 2018. She recently lost her job and is currently re-focusing on God and what He wants her to be doing.

Esther Florence

Esther Florence lives in Chennai, India, where she is a content writer and editor. She has two daughters, ages 12 and 16, and an ardent love for the Lord Jesus and His Word. She loves writing poems and Christian devotions. She loves to read and listen to good Christian music. She has a strong desire to write devotions for children and instill the love of God's Word in little children. She can be contacted on Facebook @EstherFlorence.

Sharon Gibson

Sharon Rose Gibson will equip, empower, and encourage you to enjoy the *Gift of Writing*, to move *From Stuck to Success,* and show you *How to Write Your Story NOW.* You can find all her books and journals at 15minutewriter.com/books. She has been published in bestselling books such as the *Chicken Soup* series. Her missionary parents raised her in Africa, and she has adopted seven teenagers from poverty backgrounds. She also loves to do creative lettering and watercolor.

Jaime Hampton

Jaime Hampton lives in Southcentral Alaska with her husband and three children. She has been involved with ministry to children and youth for over twenty years. Jaime writes Christian nonfiction and has a passion for studying the Bible. She also enjoys camping with her family, roasting (and drinking!) coffee, and the crazy life that comes with being a hockey mom.

Sharon Hazel

Sharon Hazel has always been actively involved in her local church, with a love for Bible study and sharing from God's Word with different groups. She is a wife and mother of two grown-up sons and is embracing a new season of her life as a fledgling writer. Sharon receives inspiration from the beauty of the coastline where she lives in Wales and blogs at Limitless-Horizon.com. Competing for her time is one very patient husband, a horse, two Jack Russell dogs, and a newly developed interest in gardening.

Jamie Kupkovits

Jamie Kupkovits is a mother, educator and the author of Relational Aggression in Girls. She enjoys reading and writing about how the grace of God has dramatically impacted her life. You can learn more about Jamie at MissonOutreachMomServingChrist.wordpress.com.

Laura J. Marshall

Laura J. Marshall works a full-time job, runs several small businesses, is an author, and has been raising five sons for almost a quarter of a century. She's tired of where she's wandered and is coming back to the heart of Jesus.

Dr. Wemi Omotosho

Wemi Omotosho, PhD is a London-based writer who wears many hats as a scientist, entrepreneur, wife, and mom. She is active in her local church as a vocalist in the worship team, a Bible study writer, and a coordinator for the publicity department. In her downtime, she can usually be found with her nose in a book or writing. Her writings have appeared in (in)courage, Iridescent, Awake Our Hearts and Kindred Mom. She is in constant awe of God's love for her despite her mess and shares her reflections and poems at ReflectionsInTheMess.com.

Dr. Karen Michelle Ricci

Dr. Karen Michelle "Shelly" Ricci is down to earth but kingdom minded. Her desire is to speak to the heart of the reader, regardless of age. Her background as a biblical wellness counselor, along with her life experiences, has given her a unique ability to write about deep topics in a lighthearted way. Her passion to see the body of Christ healed and restored led her to become a Doctor of Traditional Naturopathy. She enjoys spending time with her family, painting, and music.

Valerie Riese

Valerie suffered through years of debilitating anxiety brought on by infertility, vision loss, and breast cancer until she learned that victory over anxiety comes only through surrender to Jesus. Now she helps women overcome anxiety through faith as Co-Director of Candidly Christian. She is also a freelance devotional writer, proofreader, and editor. She lives in Wisconsin with her husband and teenage daughter. You can learn more about Valerie at valerieriese.com

Jessica Schneider

Jessica is a writer who desires for women to know that they are loved by a faithful God, and hopes to encourage them in their walks with Christ. Coffee, chocolate, and pink roses are her love languages, and she will use any excuse possible to make cupcakes. But above all, she has a deep love for Christ, and a desire to follow where He will lead. Jessica currently lives in Norwalk, CT with her husband Mike, and two children, Charlie and Olivia.

Pamela A. Taylor

Pamela A. Taylor is passionately in love with Jesus Christ and delights in walking with Him daily. Her greatest joy has been providing for and raising her two adult children. As a result of being a single, homeschooling mom and former missionary to third world countries, Pamela discovered her gifts for teaching, discipling, and writing. She is now a Christian life coach and Living Your Strengths Mentor. You can find out more about Pamela and connect with her online at LoavesAndFishesCoaching.com.

Hadassah Trev

Hadassah is a Christian writer, blogger, and a bilingual poet. She writes a blog to encourage the readers to keep moving in the journey of faith and walk deeper with God. She is writing on different topics of Christian living, focusing on the practical implications of the Christian faith, spiritual growth, and biblical guidance and encouragement. She is a regular contributor to the faith-based site DevotableApp and COMPEL Training member. Hadassah is a Bulgarian living in Austria. She loves diving deeper into the Word of God and enjoys reading, traveling and spending time with her family and friends. You can find her online by visiting OnTheWayBG.com.

Leisa Williams

Leisa is a teacher who lives in Canberra, Australia with her husband and her family. She writes from her heart about her life experiences that draw on her robust Biblical Christian faith, and from many years of working to overcome adversity in her life. Leisa's views also come from the wise counsel and support from healthcare professionals, and her educational background, which includes a Masters of Education. She loves swimming, dogs, reading, and a good soy latte to enjoy with a friend. You can learn more about Leisa's story through her book *Hope Wins: Overcoming Feelings of Hopelessness in Special Needs Families*, and by connecting online at LeisaWilliamsAuthor.com

Lyssa Williams

Lyssa Williams is a daughter, wife, and mother who is passionate about doing and being all God called her to do and be. She also wants the same for everyone else—to live out their God-given purposes. Her heart is in the truth that God can find anyone, anywhere, because this is her personal experience when she felt too far gone for God to reach her. Lyssa lives in New York City, with her husband, Samuel, and their son and daughter.

ALSO AVAILABLE

Candid Conversations

Life isn't always sunshine and chocolate. *It's hard.*

Being a Christian doesn't change that.

In Candid Conversations you'll read real-life stories from real Christian women, and how God has used their struggles to either refine their faith or used their faith to help them weather the storm. From struggling with doubts to dealing with the loss of a loved one, these women lay it all out. They aren't afraid to get real, because they know God can use their struggles to inspire, encourage, and reach others all for His glory.

So what are you waiting for?
It's time to get candid.

Contact Information

We would love to hear from you!
You can send comments, questions and prayer requests to
the following address:

Heather Hart
P.O. Box 1277
Seymour, TX 76380

Or connect with us online!
Email: valerie@candidlychristian.com
Twitter: @CandidGals
Instagram: CandidlyChristian
Facebook: CandidlyChristian

Made in the USA
Coppell, TX
12 November 2023

24114772R00090